A Comparison of a Citizen's Right to Silence Under American and English Political Systems

A COMPARISON OF
A CITIZEN'S RIGHT TO SILENCE
UNDER AMERICAN AND ENGLISH
POLITICAL SYSTEMS

Joseph L. Kibitlewski

Criminology Studies
Volume 23

The Edwin Mellen Press
Lewiston•Queenston•Lampeter

Library of Congress Cataloging-in-Publication Data

Kibitlewski, Joseph L.
    A comparison of a citizen's right to silence under American and English political systems
/ Joseph L. Kibitlewski.
        p. cm. -- (Criminology studies ; v. 23)
    [Includes bibliographical references and index.]
    ISBN 0-7734-6347-X
    1. Self-incrimination--United States. 2. Self-incrimination--England. I. Title. II. Series.

    K5480.5.K53 2005
    345'.056--dc22

                                                                                2004056599

This is volume 23 in the continuing series
Criminology Studies
Volume 23 ISBN 0-7734-6347-X
CrS Series ISBN 0-7734-8583-X

A CIP catalog record for this book is available from the British Library

Front cover: Pen and ink drawing by Carla Poole

Copyright © 2004 Joseph L. Kibitlewski

                    The Edwin Mellen Press   The Edwin Mellen Press
                            Box 450   Box 67
                    Lewiston, New York   Queenston, Ontario
                    USA 14092-0450   CANADA L0S 1L0

                            The Edwin Mellen Press, Ltd.
                            Lampeter, Ceredigion, Wales
                            UNITED KINGDOM SA48 8LT

                    Printed in the United States of America

TO ANNIE, WHO CONTINUES TO BE MY MENTOR

Said the cop as he viewed with contrition
the defendant's bloody condition
"For the case that's not sure
there is really no cure
like a solid, substantial admission."

Uviller

TABLE OF CONTENTS

Appendix

FOREWORD

This work originated as a dissertation for my doctorate in political science. However, as I wrote and examined the growing contents I perceived that this was becoming more than a research project in progress. The comparison of the laws and rights enjoyed by English subjects over time bore close resemblance to those of the United States. The comparison ended if one views the laws and rights so enjoyed by the English subjects to a hand upon which a light is shining. This light then casts a shadow. The projected shadow delineates a comparable shape of the hand, void of color. It then leaves the viewer with the ability to color it as he will. So it was with the Framers of the United States Constitution and the later addition of the Bill of Rights.

This entire document, over time, has been hailed as a "living" document, well founded in history and tradition , but flexible enough to change with the practicalities within which it may find itself. This is its true value. The evolution of time, the discovery ,through science ,of new evidentiary procedures, have all been tested by this legal and political instrument. It has not yet been found wanting.

This was possible because the Framers were able to create, out of whole cloth, a new and bold political directive. The similarity of culture at the time, including religion and ethnic background permitted such single mindedness of political thought to succeed. Would anyone be so naive to suggest that it could happen again? It would be unreasonable to believe that if a constitutional convention were to be held today that such a document could be created. The competing entities: religious, political thought, economical realities, ethnic histories, would doom such a process.

Within the document itself is the key to its preservation. Its processes, with the attending checks and balances are its protection and salvation. My work examines only a small portion of this incredible Constitution. Other emerging countries forming their own new political society would be well served to adopt and adapt as much as they can.

I have attempted to write for the enjoyment of all. The legalistic dialogue has been kept to a minimum. The historical entries help to guide the reader to better appreciate the intent and meaning of the selected "right to silence" protection.

That it has survived for over two hundred years attests to its value.

PREFACE

This book provides a comprehensive examination of the nuances of U.S. Constitutional law and a closely based similar judicial system. The variances in the political systems of each country are paramount because they provide the foundations for the umbrella of protections granted. Within each political system resides feedback controls that are useful for the indicators they employ for lawful application of the laws; specifically, the oversight concomitant with "judicial review."

It is both descriptive and analytical in its approach employing both historical perspectives and current pragmatic possibilities. Newly advanced scientific and psychological realities push and pull at the political fabric of the intents of both Parliament and the U.S. Constitution. Legal positions never envisioned even fifty years ago, much less in 1789, present instances that threaten the fairness of the trial itself. This is evidenced by the situation of a defendant with a Multiple Personality Disorder and the "right to remain silent."

The historical perspective sets the stage for the need for confessions by describing the limitations of religious and cultural methods employed by tribes and cults in their quest for answers. This progression through the pages of legal evolution demonstrates that the practitioners searched diligently for a realistic approach to determine the facts for legal resolution.

Also of interest is when the threshold of psychological stress breaches the parameter of "coercion." Where should the guidelines be located: the tolerable (legal) limits differ from subject to subject. The maturity, education and religious makeup of the subject all play a part in determining how much coercion can be considered lawful. The excursion into the early attempts at determining truth are well sited to prepare the reader for the task at hand.

The present day exposures to recent developments in the sciences is causing the legal system to include these advances in both the civil and criminal applications of the law. This book is mainly concerned with the criminal issues but it was necessary at times to put forth the civil cases for illustration. The broad legal interpretations of civil law allow for juridical examination for assessing its appropriate application to its criminal cousin.

To adequately explain the complex nature of the protection under scrutiny in a democracy, the author has attempted to integrate the most important theoretical foundations, research findings and contemporary practices in a comprehensible and analytical fashion. These findings contain such diverse areas as the use of polygraphs, psychologically created legal entities, and prescribed methods for political remedy if the law is deemed insufficient in purpose, and in need of revision or deletion. The inclusion of research into various indicators of population support, through the use of polls and surveys, assists the reader in understanding how the construction of the law, and its methods of alteration, can help the population to be protected from itself.

Extensive documentation is included for those desiring to conduct additional research in this area. With the creation of new nation states this research would prove useful in designing a critical portion of a legal system based upon political action. However, although the book is written from a researcher's aspect the casual reader will find this book to be easily understood. The legal positions are explained not from an attorney's viewpoint but from that of a layman. The information contained therein allows for those of various interests to garner portions for their own purposes.

Although both countries share a common language, in some instances this commonality is what separates them. In those instances when this might be the case, the author provides needed direction for interpretation to allow the reader to easily follow the train of the political or legal direction.

Of note are the instances of thought provoking possible scenarios that at first blush appear to be included for the sake of humor, but on reflection, they demonstrate the complexities of legal issues being interwoven by other disciplines. Human nature being what it is, critical events in the lives of citizens are dictated by the political engines driven by the populations involved. The adversarial process dictates that all possibilities be examined in the process of a fair trial. This can at times appear to stretch and massage the laws of judicial process in areas never previously contemplated. The reader will be pleased to note that many examples are presented indicating that this work was not lax in its endeavor to be comprehensive within its narrow scope of examination.

The overriding issue of importance is the "warning" or Miranda warning differences between the United States and Britain. Each approach the issue from slightly varying perspectives. Is one warning better than the other? What are the consequences of remaining silent under the two systems? Can the police continue to question in spite of the protection invoked by the suspect?

These weighty concerns should be of interest to those individuals striving to create or modify a country's constitution. Political acceptance by the population is predicated upon a belief in a document that will provide a strong measure of protection to the citizenry. This comparison, not only of political fundamentals, but the applications of its laws and their protections, are the bedrock of a country's stability. This stability then provides for the encouragement of economic growth with the by-product of a content population.

And lastly, how difficult would it be to remove this provision of protection under either political system? Herein perhaps lies the true measure of the protection offered. For if the protection declared can be voided by decree then the protection is tenuous at best. On the other hand, if the process is long and involved, then emotion can be removed from the eradication equation and reason can then win the day.

Julian Roebuck, Ph.D.
Jonesboro, Georgia
December 2003

CHAPTER 1

INTRODUCTION

Statement of Problem

This research is designed to determine if a suspect's rights during interrogation are better protected under United States law or English law.

If an individual is going to be questioned by the power of the State, is he better protected in the United States with its Bill of Rights and Miranda Warning vis-a-vis the same individual in England? For further consideration, what is the impact of a separation of powers in the United States where the United States Supreme Court has judicial review over laws generated by the Congress, as opposed to the system in England where Parliament both makes law and is the final arbiter of the law?

How the people are affected under each of the two political systems by their "rights" or "guarantees" will be of paramount concern. The viewpoint of the population is an expression of its position within the society and is an integral part of the political culture. The legal aspect of this culture is the manner in which the laws and the courts deport themselves. The population has an expectation that the courts be independent of the government and dispense justice on an impartial basis, for without this consideration, they cannot provide adequate protection for the individual in competition with the disproportionate power of the state. This protection emanates from the method by which the organized principles of the state are integrated into the legal system.

The legal systems of both countries share one important aspect of their respective legal proceedings. This perspective is the acceptance of case law or *stare decisis* (let the decision stand), whereby past judicial rulings of law are used as the basis for future judicial renderings. The continent of Europe, being easily accessible, had many impacting legal systems throughout its history. England, by virtue of the English Channel, was somewhat protected from numerous invasions of a military or other type. The United States, also separated from the rest of the western world by two oceans, was afforded a similar luxury of being allowed to develop a legal system as a normal outgrowth of its nation building era.

There are various terms and concepts which will be forthcoming, and it is paramount that an understanding of each be made to ensure proper perspective and direction. As "torture" is encountered in the research, it becomes clear that this is the beginning in defining the paradigm for the elimination of pain in the process of truth finding. At various times the phrases "right to silence" and "suspect's rights" both allude only to those rights under discussion in this research. The one additional right mentioned, although not the focus of the research, is the right to counsel. This inclusion is necessary to avoid confusion in later discussion in the research of the Miranda rule.

What this research will not attempt to do is to chart those additional "rights" of suspects in the various other phases of criminal proceedings. However, this research is fundamental to those who might later seek to examine these various other rights and thereby serves as an excellent starting point for their endeavors.

Under each system, United States and English law, comparisons of various points must be made in order to clarify the boundaries of protection each system accords its subjects. Is the right to remain silent absolute? Can an individual who is protected by the right to remain silent be compelled to give testimony against himself? And, if he refuses, as should be his protected right, does he put himself at risk? Protections granted to citizens can be altered over time through methods allowed by law under most systems or extra-legal when the law within the system is so perverted, fostering the political ends of those in power, as to be lawfully meaningless. Even though there are protections for the citizens in the law, these protections can be enhanced or eroded through the legal process itself. The citizens of the United States, with their written Constitution, have witnessed the enhancement of their protections concerning freedom of speech. However, there is the example of the legal system being perverted as was the case in Germany during the Hitler era. In the German example, the legal system fostered the political goals of the Nazi party, thereby rendering the protections provided by the law to the people to be meaningless. However, we will concern ourselves only with those political actions which would be considered lawful in the normal context of the particular problem. How the legal systems of the United States and England change their legal philosophical viewpoint must be taken into consideration, because a system that can drastically provide for, or eliminate from, its source legal underpinnings, i.e. a written constitution, fundamental grants might perhaps provide, in reality, no protection to its citizens. This legal philosophical viewpoint is predicated by political ideology being translated into political gains by one party or the other. If conservative political positions gain sufficient control in the United States government, this can now be used to change the legal philosophical viewpoint of the United States Supreme Court. This process is a slow one because the attrition rate on this judicial bench itself is slow. This change of legal philosophical viewpoint can take several years to accomplish. However, this identical type of legal philosophy in England can be changed much more quickly -- in a matter of weeks -- owing to the political structure there which can call for general elections in six weeks' time. The resultant possible change in Parliament also directly affects the laws because Parliament is supreme in all legal matters. The conclusion of this research will address this very problem in great detail in order to firmly place in proper perspective those rights allocated and the strength of the rights prevailing under conditions which may call for their demise in those political circumstances less committed to the welfare of its subjects.

The court systems themselves, of each country, vary in their assigned roles. Courts are traditionally the arbiters of the law and its applications. Although the courts are part of the government itself, the courts should be viewed as independent entities. Situations can arise wherein the courts themselves, through their decision-making power, can create law. The research will address the separate court systems on more than one occasion, thus underscoring the important roles these courts play within each political system.

A comparison of law from a political viewpoint between similar countries would be a formidable undertaking. However, if we break it down and begin to compare small yet significant segments, the problem becomes more manageable. This research will address one small, significant area of law and will attempt to determine if the efficacy of such law is better served by a written foundation in the Constitution of that country or by a steady evolution through social outlook, legal expediency or method of assigning supreme jurisdiction. Although both legal systems will evolve over time with resultant political/sociological swings of conservative or liberal goals, does one system (United States vis-a-vis England) provide for better sustained citizen protections while such evolution is taking place?

How important is a written Bill of Rights to the personal security of an individual? In the larger political dynamics of each civilization what determined the well-being of the individual vis-a-vis the political control exercised over him? When measured against the awesome power of the state, the individual seems indeed small and frail. Can a written Bill of Rights adequately protect that individual's right to silence, or is it superfluous given the current orientation of "enlightened political thought" and evolutionary "Christian charity" towards the needy -- political or otherwise?

It is accepted practice among many of the western cultures to extend basic rights to people by their governments. No one today would endorse methods of treating the population as characterized by the Nazi regime of World War II Germany. Many cultures and governments today consider themselves "enlightened," thereby eschewing those practices as physically and psychologically damaging to those within the control of the police powers. This is, in many cases, a thought; a goal; a fundamental right accepted through discussion and put into practice. But where does it live? If not in a written code, how fundamental, how protective can it be realistically considered? Christian charity is well-meaning. A written constitution may be more reassuring!

This research is significant in that the fundamental rights of the citizen must be safe-guarded by the governing political system. This allows for the orderly transition of power between political parties and lessens the temptation to wreak vengeance on political foes. With such guarantees in place, this practice demonstrates to the global political community its commitment to serve its people in an orderly and equal fashion. This then helps promote stability and as a result creates a favorable climate for business and trade.

This comparison of legal-political systems between the United States and England allows for possible future adoption in system selection for newly emerging republics to examine what effects upon the individual may be realized by either inclusion or rejection of written constitutional guarantees and the method for adding or deleting initial guarantees as future requirements are altered.

This reliance on a political science perspective defining "who gets what and how," has deep roots in the formation of legal decision-making policies. Political scientists are now showing a greater interest in police actions, judges and courts and the various penal institutions. Political scientists are also scrutinizing the decisions of the Supreme Court in the United States, the make-up of which is an ideological reflection of the political powers in place at the time of nomination of each Supreme Court judge. It appears that the various fields of the broader political science spectrum, namely public policy dynamics and public administration, are all inputting the criminal justice system at all stages. If we consider the make-up of the Supreme Court to be either too conservative or too liberal, then if change in ideological viewpoint is desired, political action across the elected officials' spectrum is needed. If the conservative Court (political conservative here being the equivalent of conservative judicial opinions rendered) needs to be changed, then political scientists will see this change occur in the electoral process, gaining governors, legislators, even the White House to help select and confirm those appointees to the Court who reflect the desired ideological shift. It is proper that political scientists concern themselves with how laws are made within the context of public opinion, relative strength of the political parties and the fringe minority groups.

This research will start with the individual's situation before it was recognized that he had any "rights" to silence at all. This root beginning will better enable us to chart the events that have led us to present-day guarantees of secured rights. Progressive case histories between the countries will be paired in those instances where direct comparison can be made. In other cases, where there is not a clear comparison addressing those peculiar points of law and their exceptions, inferences will be drawn and subjectively evaluated. This progression through the courts of both countries will reveal the political/legal reasoning helping to advance or retard that legal concept under courts' scrutiny at the time. As this is original research, the use of archival analysis allows for future researchers in this area to follow the path here taken and to add their own data and findings as appropriate to their task.

Newly emerging countries struggling to formulate a stable governmental policy amidst their own internal conflicting groups may view either or both the United States and English systems because of their inherent and historical political stability. The United States and England can provide a wealth of political knowledge not only on the practical level, but also on the theoretical approaches that are the underlying foundation for both the United States and English systems. Each system provides alternative viewpoints and options and careful study of each can provide insight to the successes or failures each has experienced.

How each new emerging nation addresses the various competing and conflicting groups within its borders, in its desire to provide a balance between an individual's rights and those of society/government, will find a rich harvest as the United States and English systems are examined. It is this framework of future political doubt that this research is designed to dispel. We have, on the one hand, the United States with its written, fundamental, legal position set out in its Constitution, and on the other hand, the English constitution which is not fundamental in nature but, rather, a mixture of tradition, ordinary statutes and political practices.

In the United States, the Constitution is the supreme law of the land. In England, Parliament and its laws are supreme. The Glorious Revolution of 1688 once and for all established the absolute supremacy of Parliament over the monarchy. This brings us to the position that, if Parliament is supreme and Parliament creates the laws, the only arbiter of judicial review is Parliament itself. How does this affect an individual's rights? Or does it?

Judicial review in the United States is accomplished by the Supreme Court interpreting the written Constitution which is supreme. However, though the words may be written, with the Supreme Court as the interpreter and with the United States Supreme Court selected by political processes, this interpretation can also be altered theoretically. As the ideological shift within the Supreme Court takes place, this shift can be reflected in the Court's decisions, either favoring or limiting the rights so delineated in the Constitution.

An analysis of the evolution of each system is therefore compelling. This analysis must be viewed from a historical perspective in order to develop fully the underlying reasons as to why each system (United States and England) has evolved differently, though from common roots.

Looking within the application of the law one must therefore utilize legal cases and studies as a natural progression of the political science viewpoint. The law is the natural child of politics. The case is made that if we wish to determine the benefits of apples and oranges, we should address the bulk of our research to the beneficial effects of each fruit upon the individual rather than examine, more than in a cursory fashion, the trees themselves. It is the final product that rests most heavily upon the individual. "How" it arrived on his shoulders is secondary to "what" has arrived.

To properly illustrate the origins of the "right to silence" we must trace its roots back through time to those civilizations less enlightened in comparison to today's viewpoint. The progress of all civilizations that have survived depicts the willingness of that civilization to experiment with, keep, or discard its various chapters of a social contract. Brutality within a brutal time of history goes unnoticed. The ancient conquerors slaughtered thousands in entire regions when they were victorious. Within this context the torture of a single individual gets lost among the piles of corpses. Nevertheless, we must move from the "thousands" to the singular for our purposes.

The very word "torture" conjures up various images of pain producing events. Depiction of individuals in pain is vividly displayed in movies of the genre. Most people flinch when they imagine themselves trying to have the efforts of torture directed to them by others. Is it abhorrence of torture that prompted the protection of suspects under the control of the government? How did torture find its way into criminal proceedings? Where did it come from, how was it ended? This must be the beginning of the research for the abolition of torture, and the sanctity of the individual is the purpose of such legislation to abandon and to condemn its use. For what other purpose could be the goal? The might of the State was now giving away a portion of its power to be vested with the subject of the State, empowering the individual, not by right of birth or title, but by right of law. This marriage of torture and criminal proceedings must at some point in time be anchored in political expediency, and the demise of its use also must have political points of reference.

The various chapters will include material addressing the difficulty the "ancients" had in determining truth or fact-finding. Ordeals, torture and their variations will help set the stage for the joining of torture and the early judicial process.

Does each legal system define interrogation, torture, interviews in the same manner? If not, then a set of definitions is called for to help the readers find their way among the various paths.

It was an interesting concept where the individual could stand his ground when confronted by the might of the State. This shows a clear departure from the interests of the State or society being paramount, to subordination of those interests to protect the individual and his interest at the bar. The interests of the State and, earlier, of the Church, were cited as reasons for the institutionalization of torture to secure confessions in cases where the evidence of witnesses was either insufficient in number to qualify or lacking in other evidentiary ways.[1] The work of John H. Langbein depicts the questions of the time in attempting to change the legal system's reliance on mutual combat or ordeals in the administration of justice and the methods of fact-finding to be employed.

According to Malise Ruthven "Torture appears to have been known to all the societies of the ancient world with the possible exception of the Hebrews."[2] He goes on to trace the earliest recorded uses of torture, by whom, upon whom, and the reasons prompting such a measure. It was clear at the beginning that State interests were of primary importance in obtaining information. Ruthven traces this position to the position of Church and Roman/canon law.

The research is, of necessity, also concerned with portions of the 6th Amendment in the United States Bill of Rights dealing with the right to counsel. The wording of the 5th Amendment and the subsequent adoption of the Miranda Warning forge a strong and inseparable bond between the two.[3]

Research Plan

Many of the sciences will allow for mathematical expression to indicate research findings. Numbers and equations assign values and the result is a mathematical vernacular term agreed upon in its research design. However, what if the research does not easily lend itself to such precise notations? What if the implied rules under research are in ambiguous terms to allow for various nuances to be addressed? Under a more pure mathematical design "a" will always represent something, "b" something different. In political science we are faced with imprecise events and varying circumstances. In political science, for example, "A" may

---

[1] John H. Langbein, *Torture and the Law of Proof: Europe and England in the Ancien Regime* (Chicago: The University of Chicago Press, 1977), pp. 6-7.

[2] Malise Ruthven, *Torture, the Grand Conspiracy* (London: Weidenfeld & Nicolson, 1978). p. 23.

[3] Miranda v. Arizona, 384 U.S. 436, 86 Sup. Ct. 1602, 16 L. Ed. 2nd 694 (1966), hereafter referred to as Miranda.

sometimes be represented by "ARZ" or "170" or a combination. Such is the discourse of political science in its very language - its vagueness, its very imprecise or ill-defined terms.

How do we assess these outcomes? The research design proposed will take into account these variances, nuances and compare them across political systems as closely as can be determined, and then view the results, and finally make a determination as to what it is that has occurred. What are the nuances that come into play when one political system advances the "right to silence" or the right not to give testimony. What is "silence?" How is it defined? And, what of "testimony?" Each condition, where possible under both political systems here in question, addresses these issues differently. If addressed differently, what are the outcomes to the citizenry so governed?

A valid method of comparing the criminal justice systems of two similar/dissimilar political foundations is through the use of archival analysis. This comparison will, of course, begin with the adoption of the "Bill of Rights" as part and parcel of the United States Constitution in 1787, and the legal dicta that have emerged as a consequence of legal challenges to state actions vis-a-vis the suspect under interrogation.

Each system was viewed (independently) from the 1787 period to the present. Major occurrences in law addressing this issue were noted in order to determine, if possible, under which system the interests of the individual or society were better served.

The use of archival analysis allowed for both the descriptive and exploratory exercise. We were then able to broaden the scope of this work where necessary and yet remain tight to the theme, thereby arriving at the conclusion and its present dynamics. The qualitative content in the archival analysis yielded definitive impressions of the value of a suspect's rights under each system.

Some of the indicators sought out in the archival process would be the discovery of methods that either, or both, systems utilized in the expansion or contraction of protections as new areas of "need" presented themselves over time. Cultural and political arguments change over time, and this impacts on the law and provisions of protection of the citizen. When challenged by such events, the research directed its efforts to determine how, and if, the protection granted was affected. Of further concern to the research was the need for implementing issues of comparative law methodology. The current debate, or the issue of contextual as opposed to textual only, serves to highlight the shortcomings. Practicality and philosophical standpoints are unequal in their attempts to balance one against the other, and the research was mindful of this turmoil when criticizing various inconsistencies of legal outcomes. Other problems in this area called upon the research to be mindful of the fact that law, within the confines of one's country, still must be viewed in a transnational fashion. This is predicated upon the concern that law is rarely a pure entity of "national law." The research was aided in recognizing this concept of "transnational" influence, because the archival analysis automatically provided a continuous stream of input across time, and this process of input, in this fashion, brought along with it transtemporal influence.

Other considerations, such as public opinion polls and surveys, aided in tracking the public's concern in those matters which impinge in such a way that political actions would be forthcoming to shape, or re-shape, protections of the "right to silence."

The extensive databases of Lexis/Nexis of Mead Data Central were again utilized where applicable to provide current court decisions on both United States and English law. This database allows the researcher to explore those descriptive areas as broadly as possible in a short period of time, thereby enabling the research to quickly accept or reject data uncovered as germane or not to the research design. Final acceptance is thus better accomplished and helps the researcher to stay focused on the research. Law libraries, periodicals and texts from both countries were consulted in fine tuning areas that required it.

Basic to each country are the laws themselves. Within the United States, various Supreme Court decisions have updated and re-defined the language of the Bill of Rights. In England, various conventions including the most recent Royal Commission of Criminal Justice 1993 will be examined.

A comparison would be incomplete, furthermore, if the research failed to include the frequency or manner in which Parliament found its own laws repugnant vis-a-vis the United States Supreme Court taking similar actions on the laws as they relate to an individual's right during interrogation, within the confines of unique legal circumstances.

How can we best evaluate the protection under the law to this individual's "right to silence?" If we can determine any inherent risks the suspect incurs by virtue of invoking this right, would it be fundamental to challenging the protection the "right to silence" should provide? The degree of erosion of this protection may be subjective because hard data addressing any degree of loss would be problematical to determine unless a trend should emerge. Other points of consideration would include the frequency or number of occurrences that either the United States' or England's legislature have overturned, or those laws they have enhanced concerning the issue. How closely defined is the protection? Are there limitations to other types of testimony that can be demanded from a suspect besides purely verbal responses? If so, what are the implications to the protection offered? What protections are extended if such demands by the law are refused by the suspect? We should note also the vulnerability of any protection in place to amendment or rescission by subsequent legislative action or judicial review depending upon the political system in question.

Terms Encountered

Winston Churchill once remarked "The United States and England are separated by a common language." It is undeniably so and, in the area of political and legal expression, it is also apparent. To assist in this comparison of the two political/legal systems, a common ground must first be established.

> The use of jargon in political science, or in the social sciences generally, has been a source of deep frustration to those -- both inside and outside the discipline -- who seek to follow the literature. Jargon arises in response to the need for precision in any field of knowledge. It provides, for the initiated, shorthand notations for whole concepts or basic elements of a scientific paradigm. If it is esoteric in excluding the layman, it nevertheless seeks to provide precision in meaning for those within the discipline. The purpose of jargon is more effective and efficient communication. The development of jargon within a discipline may be a measure of its growth as a science. The use of jargon, however, necessarily reduces the scope of communication to those familiar with its specialized concepts and to those who share a particular paradigm.[4]

---

[4] James A. Bill and Robert L. Hardgrave, Jr., *Comparative Politics* (Columbus, OH.: Charles E. Merrill Publishing Company, 1973). p.201.

The following passages will illustrate areas that could be confusing if proper identification of terms and their intended meanings are not properly defined and evaluated against each other.

British Law

Interview

An interview is the questioning of a person regarding his involvement or suspected involvement in a criminal offence or offences. Questioning a person simply to obtain information or his explanation of the facts or in the ordinary course of the officer's duties, does not constitute an interview for the purpose of this code. Neither does questioning which is strictly confined to the proper and effective conduct of a search. This was reinforced in the case *R. v. Absolam* (1989) 88 Cr. App. R 336 -- opinion of Judge L. J. Bingham defining an interview namely "a series of questions directed by the police to a suspect with a view to obtaining admissions on which proceedings could be founded."

Voire Dire

"A trial within a trial."

Where various motions are discussed prior to the actual trial itself to determine facts/admissibility of different issues.

United States Law

Voir Dire

"To speak the truth." - *Black's Law Dictionary*, 6th ed.

A preliminary examination which the court and attorneys make of prospective jurors to determine their qualifications and suitability to serve as jurors.

Interview

Black's Law Dictionary does not contain parameters for this event. "Prior to the interrogation phase - a system of free-flowing questions and answers in which the investigator gathers information from a subject for the purpose of evaluating the subject himself in terms of how the subject views himself."[5]

Interrogation

Black's Law Dictionary, 6th ed. In criminal law, the process of questions propounded by police to person arrested or suspected to seek solution of crime.

---

[5] Joseph L. Kibitlewski, "The Use of Psychology in Interrogation," paper presented at the 55th annual meeting of the Mississippi Academy of Sciences, Jackson, MS., 22 February 1991.

Custodial Interrogation

Questioning initiated by law enforcement officers after a person has been taken into custody or otherwise deprived of his freedom of action in any significant way.

Inquisitorial System

This was best exemplified by the star Chamber of King Henry VII in 1487. The Star Chamber proceedings sanctioned the examination of an accused under oath without a formal charge. It was widely used in sedition and heresy trials. The English judges gradually changed to the accusatorial system because of many abuses. People were tortured into admitting crimes that they did not commit just to obtain relief from the pain. By 1700, the privilege against self-incrimination in England was fully recognized.

Accusatorial System

This calls for the State to prove its case against the accused. The accused need not produce any evidence against himself, in fact the accused need not even testify.

Functions and Structures

The comparison of the rights of a suspect during interrogation between England and the United States takes as a given that the rulers and those governed live under their own laws. These laws and procedures are but part of the internal bureaucracy that keeps and molds the "understandings" that become a product of the culture, tradition, and political entities of each nation or state. Each in its own fashion must contain institutions that allow for the governance of its people. Most governmental tasks are common to all sovereign nations. However, it is the method and distribution of tasks that differs between countries because, whereas the tasks themselves have much in common, the manner in addressing them can be quite diverse. The most common tasks that allow for distinction between countries can be examined by the manner in which each performs the major functions of government, most notably:

A.   how political participation is achieved

B.   how political power is structured

C.   the manner of addressing the concerns of the people

D.   the various expressions of the political power itself

Those items which must be dealt with are the "functions" involved. How the functions are performed, by whom, and when, give expression to the "structure" of government.

The research will confine itself to those discreet areas which impact most directly with law-making and judicial review. This combination of political expression helps to define the importance of the function of each through the structure in which it performs its duties. David Easton addressed these issues thusly:

> There are certain basic political activities and processes characteristic of all political systems even though the structural forms through which they manifest themselves may and do vary considerably in each place and each age. . . .

> The requisite function of any political system, and the criteria by which its boundaries are defined, is 'the authoritative allocation of values for a society.' that is, the process of how binding decisions are made and implemented for a society.[6]

A look at the basic governmental structures of the United States and England immediately brings to the fore certain fundamental differences. The United States has a federated system, a two-tiered method of addressing its legal issues, whereas England's system is unitary in nature.

The House of Commons is representative in nature and contains three hundred and fifty members (Members of Parliament or MPs) who are elected by adult suffrage. It is required that a general election be held at least every five years. However, the Government can call for elections at any time. A simple majority elects its members. The representation is not proportional, giving a definite advantage to the larger political parties. The House of Lords is not an elected body being, for the most part, hereditary or based on life membership. Also included are the senior bishops from the Church of England. This House is secondary to the House of Commons. The House of Lords cannot change certain bills of legislation issued by the House of Commons.

The United Kingdom, of which England is a part, has no constitution or bill of rights. The "unwritten constitution" combines law, practices of the day and tradition, and the result is the product of centuries of government control and conflict resolution.

---

[6] James A. Bill and Robert L. Hardgrave, Jr., *Comparative Politics* (Columbus, OH.: Charles E. Merrill Publishing Company, 1973). p.221.

The people of England do not possess any specific rights but are free to do all that which is not forbidden by law. The combination of the House of Commons and the House of Lords provides for the structure of Parliament.

The functions and structures of government in the United States are directed from powers separate from each other, with each exercising some measure of control over the others. In England, the government operates with a fusion of powers. Parliament supplies the leadership and is made up of the House of Lords, the Monarch and the House of Commons. Parliament acts as the legislative body, and there is no oversight to its laws save itself. In the United States, Congress passes laws subject to the judicial review of the Supreme Court.

Political Culture

An additional ingredient of the political culture is the method by which the population assimilates its norms and the rapidity, or lack of rapidity, in changes that take place within the society. This allows for the successive generations to acquire the political socialization of the preceding generation, giving a continuity to the whole. The growing child learns from his associations within the family, school and society in general. The expectations this individual holds are, therefore, his foundation in reference to his government, and what he expects that government can, or will, do to, or for, him. With this in mind, we can then inquire of the population its opinions on governmental changes that are offered or altered. These opinions will be shaped by the population's beliefs in politics, as well as its perception of its inclusion in the nation-state and its perceived effectiveness of impacting upon the political process.

This process of political culture is difficult to quantify. Public opinion polls or surveys can provide a useful barometer of the direction the population has taken on various laws and regulations. The weak link in this acquisition of input is the manner in which the population so queried is selected, and also the selection of words used to form the questions. Bias is inherent in most types of information gathering techniques. The political agenda of the conducting entity must be included in weighing the veracity of such poll results. This research includes many such polls, and the reader is urged to carefully consider the selection of words used to convey the results obtained.

Literature Review

If we consider that an individual has "rights" in regard to remaining silent, these "rights" must have been prompted by some action on the part of the State that was found to be objectionable by the citizenry. What was this behavior and how or where did it start?

The obvious answer is that the "State" used torture to obtain information from individuals. The literature was researched to discover the origins and location of the use of torture for interrogative purposes and to trace its history into, and through, each of the two criminal justice systems under discussion.

Reports of State and Church records were reviewed where needed along with the various methods each employed. A determination was made to examine when torture was introduced to extract confessions and for what reasons. The impact of the Church upon secular matters can be traced to its policies and direction issued from the Fourth Lateran Council. This gathering was influenced significantly by Pope Innocent III, who combined his theological and legal training, political experience and wide knowledge of Europe at the time, to achieve his own ambitious agenda. The Council set down the governing position and policies dictating the day-to-day principles of the Church to be observed, as well as the future destination to be reached. Various forms of heresy were encroaching on the doctrines of the Church and were considered a definite threat to its influence. Prior to the thirteenth century, Church statutes were generally ineffective particularly in "southern France and other parts of Europe."[7] The method selected to improve the effectiveness of the Church's power was the institution of new courts which were outside of local legislative input. "The courts were to be administered by qualified churchmen instead of local bishops. . . ."[8] These courts were later to become the Courts of Inquisition. These Courts of Inquisition were conducted by a judge who presided over the proceedings. The judge heard the denunciation as well as the accused's defence and so the judge now became the accuser, prosecutor and sentencing judge. His major function was to obtain confessions, and torture was soon implemented to help in achieving this. With the temporal leader at risk in view of the widespread authority of the Church through the

---

[7] Miroslav Hroch and Anna Skybova, *Ecclesia Militans: The Inquisition*, trans. Janet Fraser (Dorset Press, 1990), p. 11.

[8] Ibid. p. 11

Inquisition, the local leaders placed their authority alongside that of the Church, in support. This joining of the powers, Church and State, gave the courts unquestioned authority. Now, when an individual was condemned, the State would place him before the Church's Inquisition for condemnation, excommunication and execution.

Miroslav Hroch's *Ecclesia Militans* gives excellent insight into the manner in which the church utilized torture to secure confessions. The two methods described in his work were the exertion of psychological pressure and physical torture. Also referenced in this work is the classic fourteenth century writing of Nicholas Eymeric. Eymeric's *Directorium Inquisitorium* describes the psychological setting and methods employed to secure a confession. The setting and method were to be sympathetic in tone to the accused, with the inquisitor adopting a manner of already having the "truth" in writing and merely urging the accused to substantiate that which the inquisitor already knew. Eymeric also describes the use of *agents provocateurs* being placed in the cells with the accused to prompt the accused into making incriminating statements. This practice was widespread in Italy and Spain with these countries having witnesses placed outside the cell to bear witness to the incriminating statements.

The State's use of torture can be traced through various governments. In traditional China, the Ch'ing Code "allowed for the torture of principals and witnesses for the purpose of extracting confessions and evidence as a normal part of judicial procedure."[9] In Greece, the use of torture was usually reserved for slaves, with the possible exception of some political crimes. If there was a political conspiracy suspected, then free citizens were also liable to be tortured. Parry's work on *The History of Torture in England* also notes that in thirteenth century France, the Crown utilized its bevy of civil lawyers who were versed in Roman law, ". . . the Roman law not only had sanctioned torture but had a procedural and evidentiary system congenial to its use."[10]

Parry notes that the Star Chamber, which was instituted by the House of Tudor, was well suited for its purposes. Its composition included "two Chief Justices, and the whole of the Privy Council, and therefore brought the highest legal and the

---

[9] L.A. Parry, *The History of Torture in England*, Patterson Smith Series in Criminology, Law Enforcement, and Social Problems, no. 180 (London: Sampson Low. Marston & Co., Ltd., 1934; reprint ed., Montclair, N.J.: Patterson Smith, 1975), p.V.
[10] Ibid. p.VIII

highest political capacity to bear on cases."[11] The views of the various courts along this path helped to determine the legal precepts for its inception, continued use, and finally the conditions that caused the ultimate disfavor of torture.

Law being the expression of political direction, there should be discovered the foundation upon which a new direction in criminal justice proceedings was sought. Further, this new direction was not defined at one period in time and held inviolate but, rather, it has been polished and bruised by the various contenders on either side of the adversarial issues at stake, i.e. State interests as opposed to an individual's rights. What defined torture? Which forms were acceptable? Were there new forms not even verbalized by the early advocates of these "rights" for suspects?

Where feasible, first editions were consulted, and review of the literature along the same paths as the research model itself:

A.   Torture
     major works in England circa 1200 A.D. to present
B.   English law -- use of torture -- change in the law 1200 A.D. to present case law
C.   United States Colonial Law
D.   United States Bill of Rights acceptance, use of the 5th Amendment/6th Amendment. 1787 to present case law
E.   Case law comparison
F.   Conclusions

This comparison of the legal aspects selected is original in nature, and so, no direct literature review can be realized. What is of importance, however, is the selection of works forming the foundation of each chapter and, subsequently, the underpinning for the conclusions reached. Original research provides the additional benefit of allowing discussion of the subject from a philosophical viewpoint, as well as providing a reference point for those embarking upon nation building in those instances where the creation of a new nation seeks improved methods of governing its people.

With research addressing torture and confessions as a starting point, the major work covering that period, used as fundamental to the scheme, was John H. Langbein's treatise *Torture and the Law of Proof, Europe and England in the Ancien*

---

[11] Ibid. p. 4.

Regime (1977). Although his work addresses both punishment and torture (judicial torture), it is the latter that is of interest to this endeavor.

James Heath and his publication *Torture and English Law* was found to be useful, as it criticized David Jardine's *Reading on the Use of Torture in the Criminal Law of England previously to the Commonwealth.* It was Heath's position that Jardine's work was insufficient in depth and erroneous in conclusions, and Heath found solace in Langbein's works. Jardine was complacent in accepting as fact that the juridical use of torture was established under Edward VI of England and lasted until 1640.[12]

The writings of Malise Ruthven give an excellent overview of torture, and his work *Torture, the Grand Conspiracy* blends well with the selected works that address the precursor of juridical torture for confessions -- the "ordeal." Because the ordeal plays a minor role in this research, much of the information used was provided by various encyclopedias with the main thrust being provided by *The Encyclopedia of Religion* (Vol. II) by Mircea Eliade. Its use is historical in nature only for its introduction of torture/fact finding, with the end result of present day guarantees to protect the suspect from such activities.

Henry Lea's work *Torture* was first published in 1866. Lea made a comparison with the archaic use of torture and contemporary judicial use of torture. He labeled it as a bridge between different legal universes. He cites how even medieval history's enlightened societies reverted to the use of judicial torture when the danger to the society strained at having confidence in its traditional legal systems. Lea was also concerned that there could be error if the use of judicial torture was viewed outside the cultural context in which it was utilized. Lea said "Judicial torture constitutes a kind of bridge between irrational and rational legal universes, a significant, if repugnant, step in that process by means of which rules of evidence . . . constituted a humanizing force. . . ."[13] This work is consulted to show the transition of political processes enabling the attendant judicial system to progress to a matter of fact genre, utilizing reasoning powers. This transition highlights the progression of western civilization and its laws from a ceremonial and negative form of proof to a

---

[12] James Heath, *Torture and English Law: An Administrative and Legal History from the Plantagenets to the Stuarts*, Contributions in Legal Studies, no. 18 (Westport, Conn.: Greenwood Press, 1982), p.xvii.

[13] Henry Chas. Lea, *Torture,* (Philadelphia: University of Pennsylvania Press, 1973), p. ix.

rationalistic and substantive usage of positive proof, torture being the bridging mechanism.

Works referencing early colonial United States judicial processes included *Taking the Fifth: Reconsidering the Origins of the Constitutional Privilege Against Self-Incrimination* by Eben Moglen. This work traces the right to silence from 1630's-1640's of England through the Glorious Revolution and into the period where the Bill of Rights was embodied first in state constitutions, and later in the Federal version. Other works such as *Fair Trial: Rights of the Accused in American History* by David Bodenhamer and *The Privilege Against Self-Incrimination Under Siege* by Mary A. Shein were also consulted, along with the various supplemental texts listed in the bibliography.

The review of the literature progressed from the origin of the "right to silence" in English law with the use of the profound work *London's Liberty in Chains Discovered* by John Lilburn (1646). The Pitts Theology Library at Emory University, Atlanta, Georgia, contained an original copy of the work, and it was consulted for the research. Other works consulted and relied upon in the bibliography were provided by various legal journals, sociology reviews and court cases in English law over the past one hundred years.

The court cases were provided by the Mead Data Central legal research system of Lexis/Nexis using the key terms of "suspect," "rights," "interrogation." This database service was selected because it is the premier source for legal research as well as complete news and informational services. The Lexis service contains major archives of Federal and state case law and it continuously updates the statutes of all 50 states. It stays current with all state and Federal regulations as well as the public records from the major United States' cities. The Lexis service includes forty-five specialized libraries covering all major fields of law practice, including tax, securities, banking, environmental, energy, and international law. The group files are conveniently set up to provide legal information from all jurisdictions and, where appropriate, add sources of relevant business, financial or general news. A subscriber to the Lexis services may also have access to Nexis service and its related services. The Hot Topics library contains summaries of the latest legal and regulatory developments within nearly forty practice areas. The BEGIN library contains ALI Restatements of the Law, ALR[R] and LEd2d articles. This makes the service an excellent starting place for the research of secondary legal materials. The Lexis service contains libraries of English, French and Canadian law as well as legal materials from Australia, New Zealand, Mexico, Ireland and Scotland. In addition, Lexis has a full complement of research tools, including an on-line Guide providing detailed descriptions of all Nexis and selected Lexis libraries, Shepard's[R] and Auto-Cite[R] citator services, and the FOCUS[TM] feature to spotlight key words in a search result, and numerous software.

The Nexis service is a leading news and information service which contains more than 5,800 sources, of which 2,400 provide their entire publications on-line. These include regional, national and international newspapers, news wires, magazines, trade journals, and business publications. The Nexis service is the exclusive on-line archival source for the *New York Times* in the legal, business and other professional markets. The Nexis service also offers several thousand other news sources including the *Washington Post, Los Angeles Times, Business Week, Fortune* and the *Economist*. It is a one-stop service for both national network and regional television broadcast transcripts in addition to carrying CNN and National Public Radio news and features. Other services used in this research were the "MORE" and "LEXDOC[R]" areas. The "MORE" command takes full-text, on-line searching to a new dimension by enabling the researcher to use a single document as a model to retrieve more documents that resemble it. The search is formulated automatically for the user by extracting key terms from the model document. The LEXDOC[R] feature allows Lexis-Nexis users to order copies of public record documents retrieved from any jurisdiction -- state or local -- in the country.

In the section on English law, we are brought up to date with the latest example of a suspect's rights as outlined in the final report, "*The Royal Commission on Criminal Justice Report*" (July 1993).

The transition of the United States colonial law of the period into constitutional acceptance and usage is accomplished by utilizing Robert Allen Rutland's work *The Birth of the Bill of Rights 1776-1791*. This work provides historical viewpoints generally accepted by legal historians. However, as the bibliography will show, it was not alone in providing information for research. Other works are cited in the research where appropriate, and every attempt was made to find more than a single source of information whenever possible. Court cases themselves provided much of the raw data. Hroch's and Skybova's work *Ecclesia Militans* illustrates how the Church increased its role in the day-to-day governing of people. This translated into a canonical judiciary outside of any legal bounds of the monarchy. The works of John Locke and the *Federalist* papers were consulted for a perspective of the time.

The court cases illustrate the change in legal thought over time from the state law decisions of the late nineteenth century to the slow evolution of the Federal position on various rights into the state legal system, thereby creating a more homogenous approach to extending protection across the country.

Major works that discuss any historic court decision such as "Miranda" were utilized where appropriate. Current cases are cited from the records of the United States Supreme Court, and the documentation for these cases is also provided in the reference and bibliographical sections.

Surveys and polls can have a decisive impact on the decision making process. As a possible predictor of political outcomes, surveys and polls give guidance to office seekers wishing to take the pulse of their constituents. These methods of obtaining public opinion, i.e., possible political direction, were examined to determine if the public has definite positions relating to constitutional issues and those political processes that help to shape those positions on such issues. The data from these surveys and polls, acquired from both countries in the research model, will help define the final conclusions reached, dependent upon examination of all the data. Of special interest here is the new "deliberative" poll now being used in England. This is how it works. A random sample of the electorate is taken from all over the country and transported to one place. This sample is then supplied with briefing materials carefully balanced to explain the problem. This is followed by lengthy discussions among small groups allowing these groups to question competing experts and politicians. After several days, the sample is then polled. The resultant survey is representative of the considered judgments of the public, in essence, what the entire country would conclude given the same opportunity to access the facts. The deliberative poll does not replace the usual surveys for it is neither descriptive nor predictive. Instead it is prescriptive. This recommending force illustrates the most likely outcome if the population were better informed.

Prior to concluding the research, a comparison of the two legal systems was called for, and usage of *"World Criminal Justice Systems: A Survey"* by Richard J.

Terrill was liberally used. Other comparative sources include *"The Suspect as a Source of Testimonial Evidence: A Comparison of the English and American Approaches"* by Gordon Van Kessel[14] for its excellent research in comparative legal studies. Although this research is similar in nature, the underlying difference remains in the caveat of which system provides the better safeguard to the suspect, and not in why confessions should be allowed.

Also of note were the viewpoints expressed by Amnesty International. However, much of the direction of their concern is prisoner treatment outside the civilian legal system and more within the confines of military/terrorist activities. The *Report on Torture* generated by Amnesty International gives historical viewpoints of the use of torture as a political control mechanism to punish detractors, and to inhibit those who may try to harm the State. This insight by Amnesty International could, at first, be viewed as outside the scope of the research if it were not for the fact that political decisions determine what is lawful. The report quotes Pierre Vidal Naquet in that "Torture d'etat is in effect nothing other than the most direct and most immediate form of the domination of one man over another, which is the very essence of politics."[15]

The results of modern court decisions and their effect on the questions at hand and determined by recent court cases in recent publications emanating from the Supreme Court, and various periodicals explaining those decisions, along with the extensive legal databases of Lexis/Nexis, assisted in the final analysis of the subject.

---

[14] Gordon Van Kessel, "The Suspect as a Source of Testimonial Evidence: A Comparison of the English and American Approaches," *The Hastings Law Journal* Vol. 38:1 (Nov. 1986).

[15] Amnesty International, *Report on Torture* (New York: Farrar, Straus and Giroux, 1975), p. 31.

CHAPTER 2
UNITED STATES AND ENGLISH LAW UNDER JUDICIAL REVIEW

Each form of government must have a deciding entity which ultimately establishes what is and what is not allowed. This final authority differs with the conceptual configuration of the government. If it is a configuration of a constitutional regime, defining the powers of the various departments of the government, its constitution and statutes, then there is a restriction upon the power of the government. Crucial to limiting this power are the courts provided. In the United States there is in place a system in which political power is limited by the courts. "Its institution of *judicial review'* allows Federal and state courts to rule that other parts of the government have exceeded their powers."[1] This separation of powers in the makeup of the Government of the United States is contrasted to the majoritarian form of government utilized in England. The United States model is a hybrid form of government "with a majoritarian executive, a federal distribution of powers among the central government and the states, and a consensual bicameral legislature with a powerful Senate, representative of the states.[2] Consensual democracies use a system of power sharing of the executive represented by the various ethnic or religious groups.

This final authority in the United States rests with the Supreme Court. In England, Parliament is not subservient to the courts in such a manner. The only one who can declare an act of Parliament unlawful is Parliament itself. In the United States an act of Congress can be declared unlawful (unconstitutional) by a majority decision issued by the Supreme Court.

If a definition of judicial review is sought, it may be described thusly: the main focus of "judicial review" is a function performed by judges and is a formal entity of

---

[1] Gabriel A. Almond and G. Bingham Powell, Jr., gen. eds. *Comparative Politics Today: A World View,* 5th ed. (New York: HarperCollins Publishers Inc., 1992), p. 95.
[2] Ibid. p. 96.

government. It is performance of judicial authority, and the manner in which it is designed is an outgrowth of the culture and traditions within which it is expected to reside. Also, judicial review presupposes a fundamental identifiable constitution. Without such a set of guidelines, judicial review cannot function for there is no basic law against which to make a comparison. England has a constitution of sorts, but it is the product of the evolution of political practices and ordinary statutes rather than one of immutable authority. It then stands to reason that absent laws which are not constitutional or fundamental, there is no higher law upon which to utilize judicial review for compliance. England succeeds in providing protection for its citizens by joining the supremacy of Parliament with a legal tradition noted for its strict observance of the law.

Although England does not possess a written constitution per se, it nevertheless operates with a body of underlying basic precepts providing for the government to be considered a "constitutional regime." Part of the unwritten constitutional pillars would include the Magna Carta (1215), the Petition of Right (1626), the Habeas Corpus Act (1679), the Bill of Rights (1689) and the Act of Settlement (1701).

This unwritten constitution under which Parliament operates also includes "common law." This "common law" is generally considered to be the practice of various customs with regard to the law and judicial decisions rendered. It is separate from legislative law.

United States

Of fundamental importance to the functioning of government in the United States is the concept of "judicial review." This concept first came into prominence with *Marbury v. Madison* (1803), the case decided by the Court with Chief Justice John Marshall interpreting the Judiciary Act of 1789, which unlawfully created new jurisdictions for the Court under Article III of the Constitution. This was but the opening round of what was to become a viable tool in the "check and balance" system of the government of the United States. The Marshall Court subsequently went on to review and overturn various state laws as well. Table 1 gives illustration to this point from the year 1789 to the present.

Examination of Table 1 illustrates several points. The first column indicates that the Supreme Court does not shy away from overturning decisions made by itself previously. This may be a function of political ideology, forces of political culture

TABLE 1

DECISIONS OF THE SUPREME COURT OVERRULED
AND ACTS OF CONGRESS HELD UNCONSTITUTIONAL,
1789-1988; AND STATE LAWS AND MUNICIPAL
ORDINANCES OVERTURNED, 1789-1988

Year	Supreme Court Decision Overruled	Acts of Congress Over-turned	State Laws Overturned	Ordinances Overturned
1789-1800, Pre-Marshall				
1801-1835, Marshall Court	3	1	18	
1836-1864, Taney Court	6	1	1	
1865-1873, Chase Court	3	10	33	
1874-1888, Waite Court	11	9	7	
1889-1910, Fuller Court	4	14	73	15
1910-1921, White Court	6	12	107	18
1921-1930, Taft Court	5	12	131	12
1930-1940, Hughes Court	14	14	78	5
1941-1946, Stone Court	24	2	25	7
1947-1952, Vinson Court	11	1	38	7
1953-1969, Warren Court	46	25	150	16
1969-1986, Burger Court	50	34	192	15
1986- , Rehnquist Court	5	4	29	3

among the voting population and/or personal positions or interpretations among the sitting body itself.

The next column reveals that the Supreme Court, as the countering force in our governing system, will also review laws passed by Congress to ensure that the new laws conform to the dictates of the Constitution, or, as the Supreme Court itself dictates, the meaning of the Constitution.

The last two columns address state and local laws with the same standards being applied to them as in the previous two instances.

The research will show the Supreme Court in action, reshaping the criminal procedural aspects of the criminal justice system. The comparison of the state cases vis-a-vis self-incrimination provide ample proof of the Court's willingness to overturn its own prior decisions to meet new expectations congruent with social engineering, morality and political ideology. The process to change the Constitution is a long and arduous one through the Congress, and through the ratification process of the various state assemblies.

England

With England, we have another concept utilizing "judicial review" in a vastly different fashion. This use of "judicial review" under English law is quite different in its scope of meaning. Whereas in the United States its usual meaning is to oversee the courts for laws for their compliance with the United States Constitution, the supreme law of the land, in England, "judicial review" concerns itself with Court decisions being proper on various legal grounds for fact of law, jurisdiction, etc., but not that the law in itself is in any way defective, because the law is a product of Parliament, and Parliament is supreme.

England does not have a written constitution. Its constitution is uncodified.

> The English constitution is a blend of statute law, precedent, and tradition going back to the time of King Henry I (1100). A large part of English constitutional law is based on statutes passed in Parliament.[3]

Parliament consists of the Monarchy, the House of Lords and the House of Commons.

> Today the most important component of Parliament is the House of Commons. . . .

> This House, more than the other two components of Parliament, represents the various social and political elements of the English

---

[3] Richard J. Terrill, *World Criminal Justice Systems: A Survey*, 2nd ed. (Cincinnati, OH: Anderson Publishing Co., 1992), p.2.

population. The major responsibility of the House is to vote on legislative bills proposed by either the government or a member of the Commons.[4]

It would appear that, up to this point, a direct comparison can be established equating the Monarchy with the Executive Branch of the United States, the House of Lords with the United States Senate, and the House of Commons with the United States House of Representatives. This comparison would not hold up to much scrutiny as Parliament's power is vastly superior to the Congress of the United States in the area of "judicial review." Whereas in the United States the United States Supreme Court is the final arbiter of the law, in England,

> the supremacy of Parliament assures the system that no English court will declare an act unconstitutional. English judges interpret and apply the law; they do not make it. The latter role is the responsibility of the legislator.[5]

So, while there is "judicial review" in England it is, for the most part, only various appellate courts overseeing case decisions and not the actual laws themselves.

This supremacy of Parliament was evolutionary as well.

> In medieval England there was no clear distinction between legislation and other forms of government action . . . terminology was confusing . . . such as "Constitutions" of Clarendon 1164, the "Great Charter" 1215, the "Statute of Merton'" 1235 and the "Provisions" of Oxford 1258.[6]

This is illustrative of the situation.

The supremacy of Parliament began to unfold. In the seventeenth century we find such wording:

> There is no Act of Parliament but must have the consent of the Lords, the Commons and the Royall assent of the King.[7]

Further, the Parliament Recognition Act 1689 provided inter alia,

---

[4] Ibid., p.4.

[5] Ibid., p.35.

[6] P.F. Smith and S.H. Bailey, *The Modern English Legal System* (London: Sweet & Maxwell, 1984), p.184.

[7] Ibid., p.184.

> That the pretended power of suspending laws or the execution of laws by regall authority without consent of Parlyament is illegall. . . .

> That the pretended power of dispensing with laws or the execution of laws by regall authoritie as it hath been assumed and exercised of late is illegal.[8]

In addition,

> The prerogative powers of the Crown were in general restricted, and not abolished, but it was clear they could be modified or extinguished according to Parliament's wishes. Other possible rivals have also been unable to maintain any challenge to the dominance of Parliament. The Reformation Parliament established legislative supremacy over the Church. In more recent times, the courts have refused to accept that a resolution of the House of Commons may alter the law of the land.[9]

A simple majority of both Houses and the assent of the monarch gives the law its legitimacy as an Act of Parliament. These acts are then the supreme law of the land.

Judicial review was not unknown to the Framers of the United States Constitution. The political scientist David Adamany posited five categories in addressing the point. They are:

A.   Framers' intent

B.   Judicial restraint

C.   Democratic checks on the Court

D.   Public opinion

E.   Protection of minority rights

For purposes of comparison with the evolution of the stance concerning "judicial review" with England's, the research has found Adamany's position to be adequate for argument's sake and that, in the main, proper foundation and equitable tolerance for each of his major points are sufficient in scope to be very useful. The research has paraphrased to a large extent his views and will indicate when the views of this research comment on Adamany's findings and whether to agree with them or to disagree.

---

[8] Ibid., p. 185.
[9] Ibid., p.185.

Framers' Intent

Although first noted in *Marbury v. Madison* via Justice Marshall's opinion, the concept of "judicial review" was far from being a novel idea to the Framers of the Constitution. The evidence indicates that it was first observed in England in the Dr. Bonham's Case (1610), this occurring during the reign of James I. The case involved the issuance of medical licenses as directed by an act of Parliament. Dr. Bonham was convicted of violating the act and subsequently appealed to England's high court, the King's Bench.

> Writing for the court, Lord Chief Justice Sir Edward Coke struck down the act, noting *in dictum*, "It appears in our books, that in many cases, the common law will control acts of Parliament, and sometimes adjudge them to be utterly void." . . . At a time when King James I was claiming tremendous authority, the court, in an otherwise trivial case, took the opportunity to assert its power.[10]

In the early part of the seventeenth century, Parliament overcame the attempts of the Crown "to assert legislative competence rivalling that of Parliament."[11] The Glorious Revolution and the subsequent Crown and Parliament Recognition Act 1689 vastly limited the prerogative powers of the Crown but did not abolish them, but did pave the way for Parliament to eliminate or modify those powers as Parliament saw fit. Having established its legislative supremacy, Parliament was in a strong position not to allow any other body of the government to assume authority over it.

The political processes in the 1700's in England witnessed the concentration of power. ". . . Authority was centralized but it was centralized in Parliament rather than in the Crown."[12] If judicial review would have remained as an overseer of English legislative authority, Parliament would have abrogated much of its long sought-after power. Huntington illustrates further by indicating that political modernization cannot take place if there is diffusion of power and a basic fundamental law. If there were these entities, then authority would not be centralized

---

[10] Lee Epstein and Thomas G. Walker, *Constitutional Law for a Changing America: Rights, Liberties, and Justice* (Washington, D.C.: CQ Press, A Division of Congressional Quarterly Inc., 1992). p. 50.
[11] P.F. Smith and S.H. Bailey, *The Modern English Legal System* (London: Sweet & Maxwell, 1984), p. 184.
[12] Samuel P. Huntington, *Political Order in Changing Societies* (New Haven and London: Yale University Press, 1968), p. 96.

and modernization could not then take place. The new concept of authority embodied, "supreme power over citizens and subjects, unrestrained by law."[13] If this is the case, we then have a nation of men as opposed to a nation of laws. Hobbes and others argued that "the Parliament is above all positive law, whether civil or common, makes or unmakes them both."[14]

In the United States a different approach was used. The traditional view, according to Huntington, embodied the idea that man could only declare law and not make it. Also, that fundamental law was outside the control of man deriving its authority as a written form or contract imposing limitations on government. This viewpoint rejects issues of sovereignty and allows for greater interaction between government and the governed, engendering a harmonious balance to permit political thought.

By 1700 "judicial review" was out of favor in England but was resurrected in the Colonies by James Otis who relied on Coke's opinion when he, Otis, argued the "Writs of Assistance Case" (1761). Otis lost the case, but history shows that between 1776 and 1787

> Eight of the thirteen colonies incorporated judicial review into their constitutions, and by 1789 various state courts had struck down as unconstitutional eight acts passed by their legislatures.[15]

Adamany further supports his point of intent by showing that over half of the delegates to the Constitutional Convention also approved of its concept. In addition, Adamany draws upon The Federalist Papers, wherein Alexander Hamilton defended judicial review. Hamilton wrote:

> There is no position which depends on clearer principles than that every act of a delegated authority, contrary to the tenor of the commission under which it is exercised, is void. No legislative act, therefore, contrary to the Constitution, can be valid. To deny this would be to affirm that the deputy is greater than his principal; that the servant is above his master; that the representatives of the people are superior to the people themselves; that men acting by virtue of powers may do not only what their powers do not authorize, but what they forbid.

---

[13] Ibid. p. 101.

[14] Ibid. P. 104.

[15] Lee Epstein and Thomas G. Walker, *Constitutional Law for a Changing America: Rights, Liberties, and Justice* (Washington, D.C.: CQ Press, A Division of Congressional Quarterly Inc., 1992). p. 50.

If it be said that the legislative body are themselves the constitutional judges of their own powers and that the construction they put upon them is conclusive upon the other departments it may be answered that this cannot be the natural presumption where it is not to be collected from any particular provisions in the Constitution. It is not otherwise to be supposed that the Constitution could intend to enable the representatives of the people to substitute their will to that of their constituents. It is far more rational to suppose that the courts were designed to be an intermediate body between the people and the legislature in order, among other things, to keep the latter within the limits assigned to their authority. The interpretation of the laws is the proper and peculiar province of the courts. A constitution is, in fact, and must be regarded by judges as, a fundamental law. It therefore belongs to them to ascertain its meaning as well as the meaning of any particular act proceeding from the legislative body. If there should happen to be an irreconcilable variance between the two, that which has the superior obligation and validity ought, of course, to be preferred; or, in other words, the Constitution ought to be preferred to the statute, the intention of the people to the intention of their agents.[16]

Judicial Restraint

It is the opinion of many political analysts and justices that the courts should defer to the elected institutions of government. Justice Gibson made an early referral to Marbury when he wrote in *Eakin v. Raub* (1825)

> The constitution and the right of the legislature to pass [an] act may be in collision; but is that a legitimate subject for judicial determination? If it be, the judiciary must be a peculiar organ, to revise the proceedings of the legislature, and to correct its mistakes . . . [I]t is by no means clear, that to declare a law void which has been enacted according to the forms prescribed in the constitution, is not a usurpation of legislative power. It is an act of sovereignty; and sovereignty and legislative power are . . . to be convertible terms. It is the business of the judiciary to interpret the laws, not scan the authority of the law giver; and without the latter, it cannot take cognizance of a collision between a law and the Constitution. So that to affirm that the judiciary has a right to judge the existence of such collision, is to take for granted the very thing to be proved.[17]

This research disagrees with the position of Judge Gibson in that the authority of the legislature is not what is being addressed by the Court, but rather the actions of the legislature as they are allowed under the fundamental law of the land. If the legislature's acts are not forced to conform to the dictates of the Constitution, then, in effect, the Constitution is being constantly amended by the legislature in the

---

[16] Ibid., p. 50.
[17] Ibid., p. 51.

everyday exercise of its authority to make law and, in so doing, circumvent the constitutional process dictated for amending the Constitution itself. If this were to be the case, the United States would then parallel the system in England where Parliament is supreme. From an ideological/political viewpoint, judicial restraint can be viewed as a "conservative" position whereas an activist court could be viewed as "liberal" e.g. Warren Court versus Frankfurter Court. Thus one can view the Warren Court as "activist" within the context of having the Court's decisions used as social engineering devices, and the position of judical restraint reflecting the desire of the Court to take a "hands off" approach in such matters.

Democratic Checks

A third controversy is what Adamany calls "democratic checks" on the Court. His position, also paraphrased by this research, shows that judicial review is defensible on the grounds that the Supreme Court is subject to potential checks by the elected branches. In various combinations, the Congress and the President may

A.   ratify a constitutional amendment to overturn a decision

B.   vary the size of the Court

C.   remove the Court's appellate jurisdiction

Adamany concedes that these checks are rarely used:

> Only four amendments have explicitly overturned Court decisions; the Court's size has not been changed since 1870, and only once has Congress removed the Court's appellate jurisdiction.[18]

This, perhaps, is an indication of how well the system functions.

Public Opinion

The fourth item in Adamany's debate is the position of judicial review in public opinion and the Court. Adamany contends that the Court decisions are generally in harmony with public opinion but that the Court really is under no pressure to do so. It is unclear why Adamany included this position. Perhaps it was to underscore a possible weakness in the Court in its desire to not provoke strong criticism from the population in reaction to a decision rendered by the Court.

---

[18] Ibid., p. 52

Role of the Court

This is the most argued aspect in the controversy: that the role of judicial review is the proper role for the Court to play.

> Those who support judicial review assert that the Court must have this power if it is to fulfill its most important constitutional assignment: protector of minority rights. By their very nature, the fact that they are elected, legislatures and executives reflect the interests of the majority. But those interests may take action that is blatantly unconstitutional. So that the majority cannot tyrannize a minority, it is necessary for the one branch of government that lacks any electoral connection to have the power of judicial review. This is a powerful argument, the truth of which has been demonstrated many times throughout our history. For example, when the legislatures of southern states continued to enact segregation laws, it was the U.S. Supreme Court that struck them down as violative of the Constitution.[19]

Under present-day English law, judicial review is somewhat more limiting. There are two basic vehicles of legal procedure. First, an appeal may be provided by statute. However, the common law does not recognize appeals as such. The appellate process operating within the common law concerns itself with whether or not the decision in the case came out of a court having proper jurisdiction. If jurisdiction was a problem, the decision could be quashed. To prevent future problems, the Court of King's Bench could issue a prohibition. Writs of mandamus were also issued to provide compliance in accordance with the law. There are two basic functions allowed for appeal or review. One is for the correction of errors of fact; the other, to provide for the harmonious development of the law.

So, within the scope of "jargon" we have "judicial review," under our comparison of the United States and English law, clearly fulfilling different roles. In the case of the United States, it is supreme while under English Law, it is subservient. The research will address how this affects its citizen protections in its final assessment.

Problematic to our study is the term "interview." In the United States, the criminal justice system assigns different rules depending on whether an interview or an interrogation is being conducted. Moreover, it is easier to describe the intents and methods of either one term or the other because their differences are so easily

---

[19] Ibid., p. 53.

defined. The setting for each is also markedly different. For an interview with a subject, the interviewer should strive for an environment that is fairly relaxed and non-threatening. The purpose of the interview is to gather information about the subject; the interviewer to provide a constant stimulus in the form of a set line of questions allowing for varied responses. The interview allows the interviewer to evaluate his subject. Interviewing is not a free-flowing, ad-libbing procedure. It is goal oriented. An interview is a directed stimulus condition whereby the responses can vary. The interviewer does not care what the responses are. The end product is subject evaluation. The interviewer is interested mostly in how the subject sees himself. The interviewer listens and observes.

In the United States, successful interrogation is a two-part function; the first being a thorough interview followed by specialized interrogation techniques. This system allows the subject to be manipulated in order to allow that subject to begin responding to the interrogator. Furthermore,

> The difference between interviewing and interrogation is that, while interviewing goes beyond a simple question and answer period which enables the interviewer to evaluate the subject's emotional response, the sole purpose of the interrogation is to obtain a confession. In the interview the conditions (questions) are constant (stimulus). The response will vary, and this must be evaluated. With the interrogation, the stimulus or the manipulation technique (only if legal) varies. As for the response, only one is acceptable: admission.[20]

The distinction between interviewing and interrogation in the United States is thus easily defined and recognizable. When we move to England, the boundaries are barely distinguishable.

The research uses the most recent legal directive for England which was finalized and presented in July, 1993. It is the *Report of The Royal Commission on Criminal Justice*,[21] hereafter referred to as the "Report." This Report was generated by the Royal Warrant[22] which in part stated as partial purpose to be --

---

[20] Joseph L. Kibitlewski, "The Use of Psychology in Interrogation," paper presented at the 55th annual meeting of the Mississippi Academy of Sciences, Jackson, MS., 22 February 1991.

[21] *Report of the Royal Commission on Criminal Justice to Parliament by Command of Her Majesty*, by Viscount Runciman of Doxford, CBE., FBA., Chairman (London, England: 1993).

[22] Ibid.

the conduct of police investigations and their supervision by senior police officers, and in particular the degree of control that is exercised over the conduct of the investigation and the gathering and preparation of evidence.[23]

The Report outlines its desire to protect or safeguard the rights of those in police custody and further indicates that interviewing (interrogation) should be performed under strict guidelines at a police station. Code C from the Report is quoted here for clarification.

> Code C provides that interviews must normally take place at the police station (paragraph 11.1), must be properly recorded whether or not they take place at a police station (paragraph 11.5(a)), and the second must be shown to the suspect for him or her to sign (paragraph 11.10). The revision of Code C in April 1991 attempted a redefinition of an interview in Note for Guidance 11A. This states that an interview is the questioning of a person regarding his or her involvement or suspected involvement in a criminal offence, but that questioning only to obtain information or an explanation of the facts or in the ordinary course of the officer's duties does not constitute an interview for the purposes of the Code.[24]

The use of the word "interview" in legal parlance here is interchangeable with the United States legal concept of interrogation, and the reader is urged to keep this in mind when comparing the case dicta to follow.

It is apparent that under English law almost all verbal intercourse, with some minor exceptions, is an interview. Of glaring importance is the list of acceptable interviewing techniques also given in the Report:

> Even when the right of silence is exercised by a suspect, the police still have a right to put questions.[25]

This last quote clearly defines a marked difference between the two legal systems of the research.

---

[23] Ibid.
[24] Ibid., p. 27.
[25] Ibid., p. 13.

If suspect invokes right to silence,

	Questioning must stop	Questioning can continue
U.S.	Yes*	No
England	No	Yes

*Questioning may be reinstituted again under certain conditions.

In the United States, when the suspect invokes his right to silence, the questioning must stop (Miranda). However, although the police in the United States must scrupulously honor the suspect's invocation of his right to silence under Miranda, the police may again initiate questioning at a future time, provided the suspect is again warned of his rights.[26] (State Holding Law).

No common expression can be used to discriminate between the two systems under research and careful attention by the reader is strictly urged. Perhaps of some assistance will be the fact that the term "interviewing" as it relates to the United States system will rarely be encountered in this research and where it might be found, clarification will follow to further assist the reader through those hazard-studded waters.

The term "custody" will often be encountered, and the common meaning here implied is that the subject/suspect realizes that his movements are curtailed and subject to the direction of the investigators. The term "custody" is of particular note in those instances referencing United States cases, for if the subject is not in custody the area of interviewing/interrogation is less easily defined and the protection to the subject under Miranda less distinguishable.

The Fifth Amendment states in part "nor shall be compelled in any criminal case to be a witness against himself." There are a host of meanings that could be implied by that simple phrase. What is a witness? What does a witness provide? Can a person be a witness who does not speak? Does a witness give testimony? Does a witness provide evidence? What is evidence? Where is evidence produced

---

[26] Michigan v. Mosely, 423 U.S. 96 (1989).

by a person? Is it only in court or can a person provide evidence, that is be a witness, in proceedings not held in a courtroom?

These nuances of evidence, testimony, right to silence, witness, etc., have been interpreted by the Supreme Court in various fashion. It will be interesting to note if the research shows, as an unintended by-product, that the United States Supreme Court views different "rights" contained in the Bill of Rights in a more "broad" or "narrow" fashion than others.

This "right to silence" -- what exactly does it mean? Is the meaning the same between the two countries or does the Bill of Rights give added protection?

Research shows that the right to silence is not absolute in all forms. Can the suspect be required to provide written exemplars thereby giving evidence against himself? Is this not protected? Is this not testimony? If so, does the suspect have the option to provide or not to provide?

Is the right to silence conditional? Can a suspect under either, or both, systems be required to give verbal information, and if so, what parameters must be in place? How has each political/legal system viewed this?

Although these nuances could be defined here as per *Black's Law Dictionary*, it would serve small purpose for it is not the dictionary that assigns meanings to the words at the United States Supreme Court level. The research will show how the meaning is stretched or limited by the Court and its overall effect upon the individual.

The Fifth Amendment also uses the word "compelled" in its body. Here again variances of being "compelled" must be examined along with all the previous "jargon."

Just as we have seen that the words of each criminal justice system differ as to "interrogation" and "interview," and that the political arena of the two countries concerned in this research also differs in the meaning of "judicial review," is it then any wonder that, within a single country, the meaning of words will differ as those words cross from the public usage domain and enter into the realm of legal definition? This point is addressed because, as we are concerned with the "rights of a suspect" during interrogation and seeing that these "rights" are founded within the Bill of Rights of the United States Constitution, it is paramount to identify how the "rights" are articulated -- what words were chosen -- what do they mean.

It would appear that more than countries can be separated by a common language!

United States Case Law and
Supreme Court Decisions

"The right of an accused person to have the aid of learned counsel was recognized by the twelfth century."[27]

The United States Constitution contains a preamble followed by seven articles and twenty-six amendments. It has three major objectives:

A.   It establishes the framework for government

B.   It designates the powers of government

C.   It protects the individual from the excess of government by ensuring that certain rights of an individual nature are maintained

In Miranda, court dicta included partial history of the thinking behind the right of suspects and interrogation.

> Over 70 years ago, our predecessors on this Court eloquently stated:
> 'The maxim *nemo tenetur seipsum accusare* had its origin in a protest against the inquisitorial and manifestly unjust methods of interrogating accused persons, which (have) long obtained in the continental system, and, until the expulsion of the Stuarts from the English throne in 1688, and the erection of additional barriers for the protection of the people against the exercise of arbitrary power, (were) not uncommon even in England. While the admissions or confessions of the prisoner, when voluntarily and freely made, have always ranked high in the scale of incriminating evidence, if an accused person be asked to explain his apparent connection with a crime under investigation, the ease with which the questions put to him may assume an inquisitorial character, the temptation to press the witness unduly, to browbeat him if he be timid or reluctant, to push him into a corner, and to entrap him into fatal contradictions, which is so painfully evident in many of the earlier state trials, notably in those of Sir Nicholas Throckmorton, and Udal, the Puritan minister, made the system so odious as to give rise to a demand for its total abolition. The change in the English criminal procedure in that particular seems to be founded upon no statute and no judicial opinion, but upon a general and silent acquiescence of the courts in a popular demand. But, however adopted, it has become firmly embedded in English, as well as in American jurisprudence. So deeply, did the iniquities of the ancient system impress themselves upon the minds of the American colonists that the States, with one accord, made a denial of the

---

[27] Robert Allen Rutland, *The Birth of the Bill of Rights 1776-1791* (Boston: Northeastern University Press, 1983). p. 3.

right to question an accused person a part of their fundamental law, so that a maxim, which in England was a mere rule of evidence, became clothed in this country with the impregnability of a constitutional enactment.' Brown v. Walker, 161 U.S. 591, 596-597 (1896).[28]

The usual discourse in examining the more noteworthy cases addressing this aspect of criminal procedure i.e. Miranda, Escobedo, *Brown v. Mississippi* will be augmented by the various nuances put forth by defense attorneys to attempt to stretch the protection offered by the Bill of Rights to cover various and sundry circumstances.

The research discusses what is testimony, and when is obtaining evidence from the actions of the accused not testimony in one sense, and just who might be providing the evidence at that moment.

With the United States cases there are dozens of such defensive tactics, some points victorious when exposed before the Supreme Court, others not.

---

[28] Irving J. Klein, *Constitutional Law for Criminal Justice Professionals*, 2nd ed. (Miami, FL: Coral Gables Publishing Co. Inc., 1986), p. 326.

CHAPTER 3
EARLY METHODS OF FACT FINDING

Determination of facts surrounding various events posed serious problems for the leaders of a clan, a tribe or country. In comparison to today, they were simple folk, their world a mystery. Why certain events took place, or did not take place, were ascribed to the actions of the gods. It was this reliance on divine judgment on which early methods of determining truth were based. One of the earliest was compurgation or oath taking. The individual parties on either side of a controversy swore oaths attesting to their veracity. Often others were involved to lend the weight of their oaths to the principals in the quest to shift the balance in their favor. The flaws of this system are obvious, and so another method evolved. Enter the ordeal.

Use of the ordeal is known to most cultures. The ordeal was the trial or judgment of the truth of a claim or accusation by various means based on the belief that the outcome would reflect the judgement of supernatural powers and that these powers would ensure the triumph of right. The word reached the English language from the medieval *ordalium*, the latinized form of the German word *Urteil* ("sentence, judgement").[1]

The Ordeal was included in various Germanic laws including *Lex Visigothorum, Lex Burgundiorum* and *Lex Salica.*

"The Lex salica called for ordeals in which the accused was tested for resistance to pain and for ordeals that involved the drawing of lots. This judiciary ordeal corresponds to the practice of inflicting torture on the accused to extort confessions."[2]

Earlier usages of the ordeal can be found in the Bible such as Prv. 16:33 "that judgement came from God," Prv. 18:18 "the drawing of lots resolved conflicts," Joshua 7:14 depicts the judiciary drawing of lots to discover the violator of a divine interdiction.

---

[1] *The Encyclopedia of Religion,* s.v. "Ordeal," by Dario Sabbatucci.
[2] Ibid., p.93.

One possible reason also for the use of the ordeal was the fact that decision making can be risky. By invoking divine intervention, the decision now became the sole domain of the divine.

Some types of ordeal would include fire, or water wherein the accused would be bound and thrown into a river. If the accused sank, this was taken as a sign that God wanted this individual, and his innocence was thus declared, albeit he was dead at this time. Other variations of the water ordeal had opposite demands. In other times or places, although the accused was bound, he had to float to be considered guiltless. The ordeal by fire dealt with various methods of involving the accused with fire or heated objects; by walking over burning coals, or by kissing heated irons, the absence of blisters etc. would vindicate the charges.

Also known was the ordeal by combat in which the accuser and the accused faced one another in combat, with the victor being chosen by God. It is assumed that many athletic events today are rooted in this quaint custom of ritual battle.

Ordeals of Combat

Ordeals of battle, or combat, both for political and judicial reasons are also worth mentioning. From the political spectrum we have such examples as David and Goliath and, of course, the various combat ordeals taking place between Greece and Troy in their long war. In England, following the Norman Conquest, trial by battle became an accepted method of determining the outcome for conflict resolution.[3] This superseded the legal ordeals which were abolished by Henry III.[4] This method allowed substitutes to be engaged in combat in place of the principals, "with priests and women ordinarily represented by champions."[5] This method of judicial proceedings silently fell out of favor and went unnoticed until 1818 in the case of *Ashton v. Thornton*, when it was invoked at this murder trial, at which point judicial combat was formally abolished following the trial.

---

[3] "When both appear, the accuser as well as the accused, let the accuser put forth his appeal in this way: he ought to say that he was present and a witness at a certain place on a certain day and hour and knew that the accused had plotted the death of the king, or his betrayal, or that of his army, or had assented or given counsel or aid or lent authority thereto. If he is ready to prove this as the court may award and the accused denies the charge completely, the appeal is usually decided by the duel, nor will it be possible for them to compromise the matter except with the king's consent. The accused may answer and avoid the appeal before the duel is waged." *Bracton on the Laws and Customs of England*, trans. Samuel E. Thorne, vol. 2 (Cambridge, Mass.: The Belknap Press of Harvard University Press, 1968), p. 336.

[4] *Encyclopaedia Britannica,* 14th ed., s.v. "Ordeal."

[5] Ibid.

Perhaps their heart was in the right place -- those hearty souls motivated by a strong sense of justice, who grasped at divine omnipotence through the marriage of seeking justice and obtaining information.

Through the very nature of humanity, since the time of pre-history, there has been crime, or sin and the consequent need for determining facts in order to assess or assign punishment, retribution or, indeed, forgiveness. The criteria for determining the guilt of a person, however, have varied dramatically through the ages, as have the parties responsible for dispensing judgment. Unfortunately, political expediency has all too often been the determining factor. Until only very recently has an accused person gained greater support in his efforts to sustain innocence, at least in a large part of the world.

Those in a position to make the determination could very often be on shaky political ground, and a misstep in judgment could have drastic effects upon the decision maker. It is easy to recognize the dilemma. It is not reasonable to assume that everyone will tell the truth about a particular event, when the knowledge of that event would not be in the best interests of certain parties. But society must have a mechanism to deal with occurrences if stability within the group is to be a reality.

The research will show that, even after thousands of years, certain obstacles still remain. Some areas are still uncharted waters, and some methods still leave much to be desired in obtaining the truth of the matter. Kings have faced the dilemma of treason hurled at one or another of "loyal" supporters. Are the accusations true or are they an attempt by those not loyal seeking to undermine the legitimate rule of the Crown? There are the examples of religious leaders (Roman Catholic and others) using various methods to root out those in opposition to their teachings. Pagan religions were also not immune to the various practices in vogue at the time. These practices included witch hunts, lynchings, drugs, ordeals, oath taking and torture with its various nuances.

Compurgation

Compurgation, or oath taking, was one of the earliest attempts to assist in the decision making process. These early proceedings do not share much in common with modern day trials. Evidence as we know it was not presented, weighed carefully, with the resultant outcome predicated upon such evidence. Compromise was also not a usual outcome. The decision was clearly defined with one side "right" and the other "wrong." The person levying the charge usually prevailed because he was the one who bore the burden of proof and therefore directed the course of events leading up to a decision.

Compurgation involved a considerable amount of minute procedures and, as long as these were met by the accuser, a favorable outcome was his reward. This was not always the case with the ordeals, nor with judicial combat. This ancient system of negative proofs "worked" for the society because of its reliance on the judgment of God to produce the guilty party.

This "wager of law" as it was called in English law, consisted of an accuser furnishing the court sufficient proof of the righteousness of his case by taking upon himself an oath. Other compurgators, who might be friends and neighbors, would then swear an oath to his allegations being true. The number of oath takers would increase with the greater gravity of the charge. There is no record of oath taking being used in those instances where guilt was obvious. Allowing the accused to take the oath was the prerogative of the political figure/judge conducting the proceedings and such allowance of this method of trial assured acquittal. There were efforts made to limit abuse of this system. If an accuser somehow lost his case, his fellow compurgators risked "losing a hand" as perjurers. The revival of Roman Law in about the 12th century started the demise of this practice. By 1300 it had all but disappeared from France. It was formally abolished in England in 1833.

If we consider ordeals we find they can be divided into three categories: judicial combat, divination and the physical test. There is the ordeal of divination such as the one used by the ancient Burmese people. In this example, the two contesting parties are each given a candle of identical length. The candles are lighted simultaneously; the owner of the candle that outlasts the other is considered to have won his cause. Divination was known also in medieval Europe. It was called the ordeal of the bier and it was predicated upon the belief that a sympathetic action of the blood of the corpse would cause it to flow at the touch or nearness of the accused murderer, thereby signifying his guilt.

"O gentlemen, see, see! dead Henry's wounds
Open their congeal'd mouths, and bleed afresh!" Shakespeare (Richard III. Act 1, Scene 2).

Other methods of divination involve the use of a curse. Water or bread or cheese might be cursed with a magical penalty wherein the accused takes the object into his body and an allotted period of time is allowed to pass in order to determine guilt or innocence. A period of three weeks was usual. Poison ordeals also fall into this category, and with the mixture and its strength being determined by the priest or tribal doctor, he thereby possessed great influence in many matters. Truth or fact finding in this situation had a great deal of human influence -- bias!

The third method of ordeal was the physical test, usually of fire or water, and this was the most common test used by the various cultures. In Hindu codes, the spouse of the husband could be required to pass through fire to prove her fidelity to her jealous husband. If she exhibited traces of burning, it was regarded as proof of her guilt.

There were burning liquid ordeals or molten metal, where the party to be tested immersed his hand to retrieve some article from the heated medium. Escaping injury to the immersed portion of the body was indicative of innocence. The Code of Hammurabi used flowing water. The accused was thrown into the water and was "adjudged guilty if the water bore him away."[6] Variations on the water theme included ducking the accused which was used to locate witches. In India one variation was to have both adversaries keep their respective heads under water. The winner was adjudged to be the one who stayed under the longest.

Islam is to be noted as a religion that basically forbids all types of ordeals. The only surviving ordeal from ancient times concerns matters between a husband and wife. If adultery by the wife is suspected by the husband, he may accuse her of infidelity and question the legitimacy of her child. He does this by invoking God four times as a witness that he is speaking the truth and by the calling down of His curses if he has lied; then the marriage is dissolved and the wife must be punished for adultery, unless she swears four times by Allah that her husband has lied, invoking God's wrath upon herself if her husband has spoken the truth (Qur'an XXIV. 6-9). This is called "lian" or "mutual imprecation." This also has obvious drawbacks, great faith in Allah notwithstanding.

---

[6] *Encyclopedia of Religion & Ethics,* s.v. "Ordeal (Introductory and Primitive)." by A.E. Crawley.

Recourse to ordeal is always liberating considering the risk of uncertainty which lies in decision making. Ordeal in the religious sense reflects a system of interdependence among the divine, the royal, and the judiciary. The king rules by "divine right," sitting in judgment as allowed by law.

One has to wonder if throughout all the years in which the ordeal was used whether or not it was, to use a modern term, scientifically tested? Was there any research performed at that time where several individuals, known to be innocent because no crime occurred, were accused and tested, at least by the boiling substance or heated ploughshare method? The water ordeal would most likely have produced not guilty results. This is a rational consideration to make today, but one must be reminded to keep all things within the historical context and, given the level of sophistication in such matters, it most likely was not attempted. However, what might have been the fate of an individual who could have proven the ordeal fake? Would that inquisitive soul have been condemned? If so, by what method? Just prior to the thirteenth century, civil law started to be prosecuted with intensity. "Innocent III struck a fatal blow at the barbaric systems of the ordeal and sacramental compurgation by forbidding the rites of the Church to one and altering the form of oath customary to the other."[7]

The ordeal and torture, virtual substitutes for each other, have rarely co-existed as a rule. The laws which supported one usually rejected the other form of fact-finding.

If one considers the Teutonic tribes, this becomes evident. A freeman possessed personal independence. There were not laws allowing for corporal punishment. If a crime was committed, the injured party had broad latitude to obtain retribution. The injured party could be bought off. The criminal likewise could defend himself by the sword against his adversary. The use of torture was thereby precluded.

That a crime was against society was not the thought of the day. Crime was a personal thing. The use of the abstract theory to promulgate legislation was beyond the scope of political realities of the time.

---

[7] Henry Charles Lea, *Torture*, (Philadelphia: University of Pennsylvania Press, 1973), p. 53.

On the Continent, in 1215 or thereabouts, the Fourth Lateran Council abolished the proof by ordeal. This reliance on God to determine guilt or innocence dictated by the results of the chosen ordeal was replaced with human judges. Of interesting note is that, if someone confessed while ordeals were the accepted manner of truth assessment, these ordeals were not used to confirm the confession, thereby circumventing its own system for the determination of truth! The year 1252 saw Pope Innocent IV generate a decretal whereby the use of torture in canonical procedures was confirmed.

Providing a legal definition of torture becomes problematical because of the various possibilities that cover each case. This is due, in part, to the recognized fact that we are all individuals with varying tolerance to physical pain, psychological implications and cultural expectations. Where, along the line of usage, does something become unbearable, intolerable? Where does it produce death? The word itself can be changed to other forms: "interrogation in depth", "rehabilitation," etc. Of further consideration is the fact that pain is subjective. Many would consider a single blow to suffice for the term of ill-treatment. If one adds intensity and degree, one now arrives at beating over a period of many hours, or several days, and somewhere along the way, "ill-treatment" becomes "torture." Further, it is the breaking of the will which signals the destruction of the person as a human being that triggers human rights groups to rebel and insist on the reinstitution of human dignity back into the process. The deliberate infliction of pain is the intent of the torturer, conducted for a specific goal, generally to obtain a confession or information.

During the mid 13th century northern Italy allowed the use of torture and its codification in Roman-canonical law and utilized it as an integral portion in the investigations of the Inquisition. This was later translated into acceptance into the common nomenclature of juridical proceedings as plain Roman law.

In less than two hundred years, the use of torture was accepted from Scandinavia to Sicily, and from Spain to the regions of Slovakia in the east. Persistence in the use of torture in certain areas of Central Europe were alive and well into the 19th century. What was occurring in the 13th century was a revolution of the legal system which heretofore relied upon oaths, judicial combat and ordeals. These were archaic systems of fact finding, or "immanent justice," which relied upon divine intervention to halt or to prevent wrongs from going unpunished. After all, if God showed "the way", it must be correct.

> In order for the older system to be replaced, a number of distinct changes had to happen; an entire system of ancient and respected methods of procedure and the cultural assumptions they reflected had to be eliminated and replaced; the idea of immanent notion of effective human juridical competence and authority; and both clergy and laity had to concur in these changes. The older system of proofs gave way before two distinct but equally revolutionary procedures, those of the inquisitorial process and the jury; the ideal of a justice within reach of human determination came to be widely accepted, particularly with the creation of a legal profession. . . . churchmen and learned lay people both professed to find the idea of immanent justice repellant.[8]

This metamorphosis from the accusatorial into the inquisitorial model brought with it methods of verdict finding by juries, and evidence required, obtained, and viewed. As for witnesses, determination had to be made as to their classification and methods of acquiring information under oath. There was great uncertainty as to the effectiveness of these new procedures and so reliance on confession became paramount.

> Confession ascended to the top of the hierarchy of proofs and remained there long after the Romano-Canonical inquisitorial procedure and the procedure of trial by jury had come to be firmly in place themselves. For jurists and lay people alike, confession was 'regina probationum': the queen of proofs.[9]

It was this reliance upon confession which prepared the way for the joining of torture with the legal systems in the 13th century.

Other problems had to be faced in light of these changes. They consisted of the question of proof and the use of confessions. With all the associative questions rising out of the use of judicial combat, oaths and ordeals, these displaced methods did provide an outcome. Would these new methods be more or less risky to defendants?

What was now in place in the doctrine of proofs was the requirement that the accused could only be convicted with two eyewitnesses providing testimony and/or upon confession. It became problematic if there were only one or no eyewitnesses,

---

[8] Edward Peters, *Torture* New Perspectives on the Past Series (Oxford: Basil Blackwell Ltd., 1985; reprint ed., New York, N.Y.: Basil Blackwell Inc., 1986). p.43.
[9] Ibid., p.44.

for then the supportive allowances called for various indicia or circumstantial evidence to provide some measure of proof.

> To overcome the lack of a second eyewitness and the presence of many but never sufficient indicia, the courts had to return to the one element that made full conviction and punishment possible: confession. And to obtain confession, torture was once again invoked, but on very different grounds from those of ancient Roman law.[10]

At its most fundamental point, it is safe to say that torture is punishment, the victim being the only real decider of which term to employ. It may also be said that torture is cruelty by the State, performed by the State's designees through the efforts of the State's judicial system. We must also make strong note of the fact that, in today's rhetoric, there are those who would espouse that any form of punishment or cruelty is torture. This will not be of concern to the research. Torture as punishment for a crime that one has been judged guilty of will also not be the focus of the research, but rather it will explore that use of torture (pain) to help the State elicit needed information to determine exactly what the facts of a particular event were. The research will also show that torture takes on many roles in the quest for justice.

Some of the principal uses of torture would be its use as a tool of vengeance. With the potential to commit torture housed within the human being, it is no wonder that its selected use was as varied as human ingenuity could envision. However, viewed within this context, torture or vengeance is a much more personal, individual if one will, method of securing satisfaction. A classic example would be those who would demand that the penalty for a particular crime should be more than death, death by itself being insufficient to balance some scale of measure. Torture here must precede the execution. This urge for vengeance fails usually to surface because at the time laws and punishments are promulgated, the passion is not at a sufficient level to let the urge of vengeance rear its ugly head. Hitler was able to use torture/vengeance as a tool of power, evidenced by the types of reprisals taken against those villages opposing the occupation of their land by his armies. Hitler's use of torture showed clearly that he understood how his vast amount of authority was an effective means to limit the individual's ability to act or think independently. Hitler's

---

[10] Ibid., p. 47.

dictatorial jurisdiction was accepted by the compelling nature of his ability to exact retribution unchallenged.

There are other forms of torture which are mentioned here to assist in defining the various uses of torture. Sadism allows for the perpetrator of torture to witness or practice cruelty for sexual excitation or release. Usually this practice is highly ritualized and, upon completion, the sadist loses interest in further cruelty. The sadist is not to be confused with the individual who engages in torture for other than sexual purposes. Whereas the sadist has limiting parameters or rituals, this "cruel" person has no such boundaries and thus looks continually for methods in which to become increasingly more cruel. The *Diagnostic Manual*[11] however, distinguishes one type from the other as (a) sexual sadism, and (b) sadistic personality disorder. Thomas Weinberg and Gerhard Falk (1978) asserted that, although sadists and masochists seem unusual, they "are now insisting that they not be seen as disturbed."[12] This brings us to the question of how torture could have been accepted into judicial proceedings in order to elicit a confession. If the observance of pain, or the receiving of pain, or its infliction on others is perhaps culturally ingrained as Weinberg and Falk suggest, then is it not reasonable to suggest that this might have been an underlying factor in the acceptance of torture? An extension could be made to the vast sections of the population in the United States that "enjoy" a good solid "hit" in football or hockey, praising it while watching the hapless victim being carried off the field. The culture allows this punishment (torture)! It is socially acceptable, even moral as evidenced by the religious schools and universities that field football and hockey teams. Such vicarious pleasure may be fundamental to humans as a species. If so, then the acceptance of torture needs only a vehicle to make it socially/morally acceptable. Only the law at present denies this from happening. Several hundred years ago the law provided the vehicle to make torture acceptable. It was acceptable because it performed a public service. It helped to punish the wrongdoers by providing confessions. It was politically correct.

The Inquisition adopted torture to secure a confession. This was a powerful tool to make someone do something which was clearly not in their best interest. This

---

[11] American Psychiatric Association, *Diagnostic and Statistical Manual of Mental Disorders*, 3rd ed. rev. (Washington D.C.: American Psychiatric Association, 1987), p. 269.

[12] Gilbert D. Nass, Roger W. Libby and Mary Pat Fisher, *Sexual Choices: An Introduction to Human Sexuality* (Monterey, CA: Wadsworth Health Sciences Division of Wadsworth, Inc., 1981), p. 382

familiarity with the power of torture leads to its approval and so the acceptance of torture then leads to its justification. With this acceptance of torture to secure confessions, other aspects become evident. What makes torture so abhorrent is the fact that it begins with the interrogator committed to the belief that the suspect is guilty. This allows then for the interrogator to persist in the administration of torture until the confession is secured. The effects of torture are unilateral in that the compelling reason for the torture is to obtain a confession or other information deemed vital to the State. If this is so, then could it not be said that the State, at that time, was preoccupied with obtaining convictions rather than in the pursuit of justice.

The pursuit seems curious looking back at its path. Originally there were the oaths issued or taken at a place of reverence. Together were the accused and his accusers. The criminal was present when adjudication occurred, this in public. Then the ordeals became another public event. The judicial duels taking on a festive atmosphere with hundreds, perhaps thousands, in attendance; the customs and political culture validated by these judicial proceedings. To then allow the pursuit of justice to be transferred to some loathsome place demanded that society, ever so gently, be eased into this quarter.

As stated earlier, the greatest impetus took place following the Norman Conquest. The trials by combat then were "plenty of proof of the employment of illegal torture during these periods by gaolers either for the purpose of extracting money or to induce prisoners to give false evidence against others."[13]

The Early "Bill of Rights"

If power corrupts and absolute power corrupts absolutely, then the needs of the citizenry are clearly indicated. With the governing body being a monarchy with all its inherent power, the individual was clearly outgunned when confronted by the might of this monarchy/government.

Before we can examine the Bill of Rights amending the United States Constitution, thought must be given to that pre-history which gave birth to such high ideals as individuals' rights vis-a-vis governmental needs or desires. Although we are primarily concerned with the rights of a suspect during interrogation, some

---

[13] L.A. Parry, *The History of Torture in England*, Patterson Smith Series in Criminology, Law Enforcement, and Social Problems, no. 180 (London: Sampson Low. Marston & Co., Ltd., 1934; reprint ed., Montclair, N.J.: Patterson Smith, 1975), p. 27.

inclusion of other "rights," and when they were demanded, is a necessary foundation to the whole concept. The earliest established "rights" concerned the writ of habeas corpus and trial by jury, both of which had roots planted prior to 1215 and the Magna Carta.[14] By the twelfth century the accused was entitled to the "aid of learned counsel."[15] In 1444 was added the enactment "to release readily prisoners on bail unless their crime was of an extremely serious nature."[16]

The use of royal prerogative by James II suspending penal laws "in matters ecclesiastical" brought forth a Bill of Rights making objection in concrete form. "The pretended power of suspending laws, or the execution of laws by regal authority, without consent of parliament, is illegal."[17] However, it was John Lilburn who is best remembered for his fight against self-incrimination when he was taken before the Star Chamber in 1637 charged with printing and publishing seditious books. At his trial Lilburn said:

> I am not willing to answer you to any more of these questions, because I see you go about by the Examination to ensnare me: for seeing the things for which I am imprisoned cannot be proved against me, you will get other matter out of my examination; and therefore if you will not ask me about the thing laid to my charge, I shall answer no more . . . I think by the law of the land, that I may stand upon my just defence, and not answer to your interrogations.[18]

His defense was a landmark in that this point of law had never before been pressed to any great degree for lack of solid evidence, but his defense was later justified by an act of Parliament in 1641.

In Protestant England this Bill of Rights supported both the common and statute law. Later these rights were carried to the colonies and began to show up in various forms in the different settlements.

The research covered not only the early settlement reasons for having a "bill of rights" but also some of the prevailing thoughts addressing the issues involved in the drafting process of the United States Constitution itself.

---

[14] Robert Allen Rutland, *The Birth of the Bill of Rights* (Boston: Northeastern University Press, 1983), pp. 4-5.

[15] Ibid., p. 5.

[16] Ibid., p. 5.

[17] Ibid., p. 7.

[18] Ibid., p. 8.

The lofty ideals of justice, so proudly held by most Americans, stemmed from beginnings that were in contrast to their outcomes. Such is the case with *nemo tenetur propere seipsum* -- "no one is bound to betray himself." Indeed, the early colonial period of the United States was preoccupied with survival paramountly and the rights of citizens somewhat further down the scale of priorities. Economic considerations for providing judges and jails strained at all locations, with the distances between small settlements being the underlying cause.

It would have been of some benefit if the reporting of the legal proceedings of this period had been in greater detail, especially from all the colonial entities in evidence at the time. However, the only "qualitative reconstruction of the criminal justice system" for the period is from colonial New York.[19]

The various colonies differed in many ways -- religion, economic origins, urban and rural considerations and the various nuances borne out of ethnic diversity. The one common thread for the period was, however, "an intention in principle to provide criminal justice in conformity with the laws of England."[20]

As mentioned earlier, time and distance and economic factors eroded the philosophical trappings of the law to expose the raw essence. If an individual was charged for a serious crime and jailed until trial, the sheriff was responsible for delivering the prisoner up for trial. If the prisoner escaped, the sheriff was liable to be fined and also imprisoned. A quick trial was preferred and was usually predicated upon how soon a judge could find his way to the outlying district. It is no wonder that the practicality of the "'accused speaks' trial represented the common core of English criminal procedure in America during the first century of settlement."[21]

It is key to this period that John Langbein's explanation of the "accused speaks" be paraphrased.[22] The defendant was without the aid of counsel, limited in his ability to call witnesses of his own, and denied access to the adverse evidence before trial presentation including the charging instrument itself. At trial, the defendant confronted a prosecution who was not hindered by proving a case beyond a

---

[19] Eben Moglen, "Taking the Fifth: Reconsidering the Origins of the Constitutional Privilege against Self-Incrimination," 92 *Michigan Law Review* 1086 p. 88.

[20] Ibid., p. 89.

[21] Ibid., p. 90.

[22] John H. Langbein, "The Historical Origins of the Privilege Against Self-Incrimination at Common Law." 92 *Michigan Law Review* 1047 (1994):1060-1062.

reasonable doubt; at pretrial committal he was examined unsworn by a Justice of the Peace who wrote down his answers and other evidence, including any confession, and who then made this available at the trial. The defendant faced a tremendous hurdle at trial in trying to explain all this away without providing greater obstacles for him to overcome.

Although deprivation of counsel for the defendant was routine, several points must be viewed. First, trained lawyers were few in number and those available usually shunned criminal practice. In some cases paid lawyers were banned from court.[23] Other states had various allowances for participation including capital cases (Virginia 1734). It appears that even then a distrust of lawyers was in evidence among the various colonial communities.

In England at the end of Charles II's reign, the claim that no man was bound to incriminate himself on any charge, in any court, was generally conceded by the English judges. After 1700, this privilege was fully recognized.

In America, the formation of the various states saw this principle codified into their various state constitutions. Seeing that this was already entrenched in the common law, the preservation of the concept guarding it against legislative or judicial change was the normal progression of the thought. At the time of the Declaration of Independence, five of the original thirteen colonies included this as a part of their developed constitutions.

---

[23] Eben Moglen, "Taking the Fifth: Reconsidering the Origins of the Constitutional Privilege against Self-Incrimination," 92 *Michigan Law Review* 1086 p. 91.

CHAPTER 4
THE RIGHT TO SILENCE UNDER UNITED STATES LAW

There are several areas that invite comparison. They are:

A. The strict usage of the right to silence/no compulsion to self-incriminate

B. Early interpretations

C. Miranda and Escobedo

D. State compelled self-incrimination

E. Public expectations of the Government

F. Use of psychology in interrogations

G. Immunity

H. Multiple personalities

I. Miranda and its effects

The major cases under both systems (United States and English) will be analyzed and compared, as the inclusion of all possible exceptions would cause the research to become unmanageable and would serve little purpose.

For the case of the United States protection, in the first instance, reliance upon *Miranda v. Arizona* seems the most justified for its precedent-setting and for exploration in the delivered dicta of the rights and protections.

It would do the reader well to keep in mind how the Supreme Court affixes strict interpretations upon some provisions of the Bill of Rights while broadening the inclusion of others i.e. the First Amendment and Fourth Amendment. Although not the focus of the research, this causes the reader to wonder why the disparity does in fact exist!

The Bill of Rights was added to the United States Constitution to protect the individual from the power of the government, in this case the Federal Government. Most state constitutions of the time already had their "Bill of Rights" protecting the individual from the state governments. Not envisioned by these geniuses of political thought and protectors of individual liberty were the advances of technology into areas not even within their dreams. The Fifth Amendment to the United States

Constitution states in part, ". . . nor shall any person be subject for the same offence to be twice put in jeopardy of life or limb; nor shall be compelled in any criminal case to be a witness against himself." The protection seems to be crystal clear. However, the following cases will illustrate that the crystal has many "facets" to its clarity.

Non-Testimonial Self-Incrimination

If someone commits a crime he should be held accountable. The evidence against him placed before a lawful tribunal is a setting providing for a fair trial. He should not be tortured nor threatened with punishment should he refuse to provide evidence against himself. The government in its quest to prosecute must do so on the evidence obtained by its own resources rather than through the compelled assistance of the accused.

Although this appears to be a solid principle founded upon the Constitution, there are many cases in which this protection has been eroded. An accused may be required to participate in a line-up,[1] to provide writing exemplars,[2] to declare the use of any aliases,[3] to walk a particular way,[4] etc. Provision of the aforementioned cannot be denied as anything but giving evidence -- incriminating and most damning for the most part -- with refusal to provide such testimony, evidence, etc. not being an option. The Supreme Court, in all its wisdom, has declared that providing such evidence is not "testimonial," therefore it falls outside the protection granted by the Fifth Amendment. An examination of the several noted cases is called for in order to grasp the fundamental position of the various state courts in assessing its position to the "rights" under protection. As for the position of the Supreme Court in these cases, the research will examine the various positions both in the comparisons phase and the conclusion argument.

Although provided for from the time of the acceptance of the Bill of Rights, the claim not to self-incriminate was, for the most part, confined to the trial phase of the criminal proceedings against an accused. The argument against strict observance of the words of the Fifth Amendment is well discovered through the article written by

---

[1] United States v. Wade, 388 U.S. 218 (1967).
[2] Gilbert v. California, 388 U.S. 263 (1967).
[3] United States v. Prewitt, 553 F. 2d 1082, 1085-96 (7th Cir. 1977).
[4] Hill v. State, 366 So. 2d 318 (Ala. 1979).

Charles Gardner Geyh, "The Testimonial Component of the Right against Self-Incrimination."[5]

To place a better perspective on the present position of the Court, it is necessary to indicate that prior to *Schmerber v. Calif.* (1966) it was generally held by the Court that the privilege against self-incrimination was broadly interpreted. The following is a partial list of selected cases which give fair indication of the Courts' position. Of note is the year represented for each.

> By the weight of authority it is held to be error to compel the accused to submit to a comparison of footprints and to permit a witness who was present when the accused was forcibly compelled to place his foot in footprints, or to surrender his shoes for the purpose of making a comparison, to testify as to the result . . . *State v. Sirmay*, 40 Utah 525, 537, 122 P. 748, 753 (1912)

> *Cooper v. State*, 86 Ala. 610, 6 So. 110 (1889) (admission of evidence that defendant refused to make tracks in his stocking feet for comparison purposes was reversible error).

> *Day v. State*, 63 Ga. 667 (1879); *State v. Griffin*, 129 S.C. 200, 124 S.E. 81 (1924); *Stokes v. State*, 64 Tenn. 619 (1875)

> further, *People v. Akin*, 25 Cal.

> App. 373, 143 P. 795 (1914); *State v. Horton*, 247 Mo. 657, 153 S.W. 1051 (1913) (Reversible error to compel accused to undergo physical examination); *Bowers v. State*, 45 Tex. Crim. 185, 75 S.W. 299 (1903); *Whitehead v. State*, 39 Tex. Crim. 89, 45 S.W. 10 (1898).

> *State v. Jacobs*, 50 N.C. 259 (1858) (defendant cannot be compelled to exhibit himself as a means to establish that he is a free negro); *Blackwell v. State*, 67 Ga. 76 (1881) (it was error to compel the defendant to exhibit his leg); *State v. Garrett*, 71 N.C. 85, 87 (1874) (impermissible to compel an accused to unwrap a bandage and exhibit a wound; once done, however, a witness' testimony concerning the wound was admissible).

> *Aiken v. State*, 16 Ga. App. 848, 86 S.E. 1076 (1915) (it was error to compel defendant to stand in a window for identification).

Other cases of note:

---

[5] Charles Gardner Geyh, "The Testimonial Component of the Right against Self-Incrimination," 36 *The Catholic University Law Review* 611 (Spring 1987).

People v. Mead, 50 Mich. 228, 15 N.W. 95 (1883) (a prisoner cannot be required to measure or try on a shoe; it is permissible, however, if he does so voluntarily); *Gallagher v. State*, 28 Tex. App. 247, 281, 125 S.W. 1087, 1095 (1889) (no violation of right where defendant voluntarily dons a hat and mask; however, "if in his case, the defendant had declined to be distinguished and exhibited, the court would doubtless have protected him in his constitutional right to be exempted from giving evidence against himself"); *Turman v. State*, 50 Tex. Crim. 7, 95 S.W. 553 (1906) (defendant cannot be compelled to put a cap on his head); *Ward v. State*, 27 Okla. Crim. 362, 228 P. 498 (1924) (defendant may not be compelled to put on a coat); *Reyes v. Municipal Court*, 41 P.R. 892 (1931) (defendant may not be compelled to dishevel his hair and pull down his cap).

Counter argument to this position views that the protection offered is founded in the determination of truth. Whereas verbal communication can be unreliable, confessions etc. can be fabricated to achieve some ulterior motive.

Of note, however, is the dissenting opinion of Justice J. Brennan in *California v. Byers*.[6] Justice Brennan held that the protection of the Fifth Amendment included "non-testimonial compulsion" but that this protection of the accused was overridden by the government's interest in conducting the criminal process in an orderly and efficient manner.

The earlier cases offered were from the various state courts as the Supreme Court had not yet incorporated the Bill of Rights into the Fourteenth Amendment making the Federal provisions applicable to the state judicial systems. However, if we look at these state cases closely we can see that it was their intent to incorporate a broader view of the protection against self-incrimination as their own state constitutions, many of which pre-dated the United States Constitution, called for such broad provisions. The incorporation broached the federal/state separation, and what remains is the Federal system of procedural provisions in state criminal proceedings and leaves intact essentially the state substantive law.

The Supreme Court looks at this issue on a Federal level in *Holt v. United States* (1910).[7] The case centered around the accused being "compelled" to wear a blouse to see if it fitted him. The accused was appealing on the grounds that the same duress that would make his statements inadmissable should also exclude his

---

[6] California v. Byers, 402 U.S. 424, 464-65, 473-74 (1971).
[7] Holt v. United States, 218 U.S. 245 (1910)

wearing of the blouse. The reasoning of the Court with its contrary holding was based upon the position that if his assertion was valid, it would then invalidate the compelling of the accused to present himself in court for identification. It appears that this Court relied heavily upon the legal writings of John Wigmore.

Appearing in court dressed as the defendant would like to be does not equate to his being dressed as the State would like him to be -- nor would the defendant's utterances have to be the same as what the State would like, i.e confession, etc. He can speak without giving a confession as the words are his -- being dressed by the prosecution is different!

So, two issues contributed to this dichotomy of judicial viewpoints. One, the states' judicial system was not subservient to the Federal system which embraced the Bill of Rights in its proceedings and, two, the United States Supreme Court's reliance on the writings of John Wigmore which narrowly interpreted the protection offered. Again, it is of some importance to know how Wigmore would have positioned himself in regard to the protections outlined in the First Amendment.

Also to be taken into consideration at this time was the general make-up of the United States Supreme Court. It was generally composed of those lawyers whose expertise in business/commercial pursuits brought them the political favor to be appointed to the august body they inhabited.

Law enforcement was still pretty much in the neophyte stage, with the first police academy appearing at the turn of the century, a mere seventy odd years after the first dedicated police departments were organized.

Miranda and Escobedo

The advent of the 1960's and the activism of the Warren Court heralded a new initiative by the Supreme Court to use the Fourteenth Amendment to impose Federal judicial standards upon the various states. Whereas the protection afforded to the citizen might vary in state courts, the Supreme Court, through appellate state actions to the Federal level, sought to standardize the manner in which the procedural aspects of the criminal justice system would conduct its affairs. This period saw many state actions declared unconstitutional if they were found to be contrary to Federal guidelines for Federal prosecution. The case of *Mapp v. Ohio*[8] helped to remove the

---

[8] Mapp v. Ohio, 367 U.S. 643, 655 (1961).

old "silver platter" doctrine wherein evidence, which would have been illegally obtained under Federal guidelines and therefore useless in Federal Court, could be obtained under state guidelines and given to the Federal Court on a "silver platter," was allowed then to be admissible. This new guideline known as the "exclusionary rule" prevented the use and the derivative use of any evidence seized in violation of the Fourth Amendment. Other procedural questions concerning rights to an attorney and when those rights were deemed important to the suspect, as they relate to the respective proceedings from investigation through completion of any sentence after trial, were given the force of law by the liberal Supreme Court empaneled at the time.

The earliest requirement imposed by the United States Supreme Court on confessions addressed the point of voluntariness. Was the confession freely given? Two cases which concerned this aspect added their name to a rule of examination known as the McNabb-Mallory Rule: Supervisory Authority over Federal Justice versus Fourteenth Amendment Due Process.

Prior acknowledgement or admissibility of a confession was predicated that it be free of influence which may make it untrustworthy. Dean Wigmore disagreed with the concept that used the word "voluntary" for the reason "there is nothing in the mere circumstance of compulsion to speak in general . . . which create any risk of untruth."[9] But voluntariness remained an issue.

In 1936, the Supreme Court threw out the confession in *Brown v. Mississippi*[10] determining that a confession obtained after a severe beating presided over by deputies interfered with the integrity of the fact-finding process.

In *Ashcraft v. Tennessee*[11] the Supreme Court reversed a conviction based upon a confession obtained after thirty-six hours of interrogation. The Court's position was that prolonged interrogation amounted to "coercion." This position by the Court "reflected less a concern with the reliability of a confession as evidence of guilt in the particular case than disapproval of police methods which a majority of the Court conceived as generally dangerous and subject to serious abuse."[12]

---

[9] Yale Kamisar et al., *Basic Criminal Procedure*, (St. Paul, MN: West Publishing Co., 1994), p. 452.
[10] Brown v. Mississippi, 297 U.S. 278, 56 Sup. Ct. 461, 80 L. Ed. 682 (1936).
[11] Ashcraft v. Tennessee, 322 U.S. 143, 64 Sup. Ct. 921, 88 L. Ed. 1192 (1944).
[12] Yale Kamisar et al., *Basic Criminal Procedure*, (St. Paul, MN: West Publishing Co., 1994), p. 453.

It was during the time period covered by these cases that the McNabb[13]-Mallory[14] Rule (1936-1957) emerged. This rule underscored the Supreme Court's supervisory capacity over the workings of the criminal justice system on the Federal level. In McNabb, the suspect was held over seven hours before being brought in front of a committing magistrate. During this seven-hour period, the suspect gave incriminating statements to the police. Although this seven-hour delay was not in violation of state law, it was deemed to be in violation of Federal law. The Court concluded that the incriminating statements, although voluntary, were obtained during unlawful detention according to Federal standards and therefore rendered the use of the statements in a Federal trial unacceptable. This rule "was heavily criticized by law-enforcement spokesmen and many members of Congress. . . ."[15] In Mallory, the Court emphasized the point that there should be no unnecessary delay in bringing the detainees before a committing magistrate. This rule, although adopted by several states, was not placed upon the states by the Court through the Fourteenth Amendment. What took its place was the Court's continued insistence to the right to counsel and the privilege of self-incrimination. The outcome witnessed the states' rules governing confessions to exceed the McNabb-Mallory requirements.

It was little wonder that the area of confessions and their admissibility would take their allotted place before the United States Supreme Court for re-examination. It started with *Escobedo v. Illinois*.[16] In this case, Escobedo was arrested and released on a writ of habeas corpus. He made no statements at this time. Eleven days later he was arrested. Before making any statement, he requested his attorney for consultation and was denied access to his attorney. His attorney was, at the same time, trying to reach his client but was told by the police that access would be denied until after the police conducted their interrogation. Escobedo admitted knowledge of the crime and was convicted. The Supreme Court reversed the conviction on appeal stating, "The post arrest interrogation was the stage when legal aid and advice were most critical." (Mr. Justice Goldberg). With the Escobedo decision, the right to counsel was extended to the earliest possible moment in the criminal process.

---

[13] McNabb v. United States, 318 U.S. 332, 63 Sup. Ct. 608, 87 L. Ed. 819 (1943).
[14] Mallory v. United States, 354 U.S. 449, 77 Sup Ct. 1356, 1 L. Ed. 2d. 1479 (1957).
[15] Yale Kamisar et al., *Basic Criminal Procedure*, (St. Paul, MN: West Publishing Co., 1994), p. 459.
[16] Escobedo v. Illinois, 378 U.S. 478, 488-491 (1964).

Where Escobedo opened the door to provide Federal protection in state criminal cases, Miranda attached the Fifth Amendment to that of the Sixth Amendment and Escobedo.

The Miranda warning is widely known to program watchers of police dramas. The suspect is apprehended and a law enforcement officer starts to read "You have the right to remain silent . . . ." This was not always the case. Here is how it came to pass. Ernesto Miranda was arrested on March 13, 1963 for kidnapping and rape. He was taken to a police station in Phoenix, Arizona. Without being advised of his rights, Miranda was interrogated for two hours, after which time he signed a written confession. The top portion of his written statement contained a paragraph which said the statement was voluntarily given and that no threats or promises of immunity were invoked and "with full knowledge of my legal rights, understanding any statement I make may be used against me."[17] Essentially, the Supreme Court held that Miranda was not advised of his rights *prior* (author's emphasis) to making an oral confession which preceded the written version, he was not advised of his right to have an attorney to consult with prior to making any statement or that he had a right to have an attorney present during any questioning, nor that he had a right not to be compelled to incriminate himself. The Court also held, in reversing his conviction, that although the written statement contained a typed-in clause stating that he had "full knowledge" of his "legal rights" this did not demonstrate that he was intelligently and knowingly waiving his constitutional rights.

The court did not say that statements made by the accused are not admissible. What has evolved is a set of conditions that must be met before the admission or confession can be used as evidence. They are:

A.   It must pass the traditional test of voluntariness and trustworthiness

B.   It must meet the requirements of *McNabb v. United States*[18] and *Mallory v. United States*[19]

C.   It must meet Miranda requirements

D.   It is possible to taint a confession by an illegal search or seizure

E.   Failure to provide counsel may also invalidate a confession

---

[17] Miranda v. Arizona, 384 U.S. 436, 86 S. Ct. 1602, 16 L. Ed. 2nd 644 (1966).

[18] McNabb v. United States, 318 U.S. 332, 63 S. Ct. 608, 87 L. Ed. 819 (1943).

[19] Mallory v. United states, 354 U.S. 449, 77 S. Ct. 1356, 1 L. Ed. 2d 1479 (1957).

The decision in Miranda was not unanimous. There were four dissenters who stated that the majority opinion was not supported by either history or the wording of the Fifth Amendment. It was the position of the dissenters that the privilege against self-incrimination, as developed at common law, prohibited only compelled *judicial* interrogation. Also, they could find no authority for extending the privilege to out-of-court confession but they did agree that the test for voluntariness should be retained. An illegal search can taint a confession so as to make it inadmissible. If items are seized in an illegal search and the suspect, subsequently arrested and interrogated, gives a voluntary confession, the fact that the confession was a result of the illegal search would be cause to dismiss the confession as well as the illegally seized items. Escobedo showed how serious failures to allow/provide counsel can be in viewing the admissibility of ensuing confessions.

State Compelled Self-Incrimination

What is of interest here is that the word "compelled" again becomes important. In the cases of *Wade* and *Gilbert*, the suspect was compelled in helping the State gather evidence which was incriminating. If this point is to be disregarded as non-testimonial, then the question is begged as to whether or not compelling a suspect to perform or provide certain information or samples is testimonial in nature, for if the accused can be compelled to provide the evidence sought, the very act of providing the evidence is testimonial in nature. Whereas the evidence itself may be non-communicative or non-testimonial, the fact that the accused did in fact produce it is testimonial in itself. However, a witness does provide more than testimonial evidence. Take for example a laboratory chemist who performs certain tests. The tests provide evidence without which the testimony would be useless. However, at trial the witness gives validity to the test results. Without such testimony it is unlikely that the test results would be admitted into evidence. With the compelling of the accused to perform certain acts, deeds, or to supply biological samples, we have a situation that again changes the rules for the submission of evidence. The argument is two-fold with the second part being the convenient overlooking of the "compelling" nature of the state's right to acquire certain evidence from the "self" involved i.e. the accused.

It is in this regard that the position of John Wigmore is at odds with the Constitutional protection. Wigmore's position is paraphrased thusly. The individual's protection against self-incrimination was limited to using the legal process in order to extract an admission of his guilt from that individual's own lips. It appears the extraction of information from the lips is prohibited to the state but the extraction of information from the accused's veins is fair game! But Wigmore carried on to justify his position on three points. In the first place:

> The process of the ecclesiastical [c]ourt, as opposed to through two centuries, . . . the inquisitorial method of putting the accused upon his oath, in order to supply the lack of the required two witnesses.[20]

It would appear that the straightforward requirement of yesteryear of two witnesses has been supplanted by laboratory technicians, handwriting experts and others of the forensic craft. His second reasoning for justification concerned the policy of the position as a defensible institution which, in Wigmore's view, was simply to impress upon the prosecution the need for them to obtain evidence strictly through their own efforts. But the prosecution, now so stimulated, still looks to the accused to provide evidence in the main which then is processed by the prosecution's experts in the various forensic fields to discover what evidence has been yielded, or better, "compelled" from the accused. Wigmore's third and final justification for limiting the scope of self-incrimination was "the practical requirement that follows from the necessity of recognizing other unquestioned methods of procuring evidence."[21] Wigmore's support hinged on his argument the "self," and it is most important to note that Wigmore strays from the "self" to include "self" plus "physical control." "If the privilege afforded protection not only for the suspect's physical control of his own vocal utterances, but also for his physical control in whatever form exercised" then Wigmore concluded that it would be possible for a guilty person to shut himself up in his house, with all the tools and indicia of his crime, and defy the authority of the law to employ in evidence anything that might be obtained by forcibly overthrowing his possession and compelling the surrender of the evidential articles, in a clear reduction *ad adsurdum*. Again, Wigmore failed to note that the law has the authority to search and seize articles under the procedural guidelines of the Fourth Amendment. Seizure is not forbidden as he would suggest, just regulated in its form.

---

[20] Charles Gardner Geyh, "The Testimonial Component of the Right against Self-Incrimination," *36 Catholic University Law Review* 611 (Spring 1987):63
[21] Ibid., p. 63.

Further, "possession" is not mentioned in the Fifth Amendment, though a weak case could be made that the accused possesses his biological fluids, handwriting, etc., but this argument fails to hold if "knowledge" is considered a possession as well. Not only that but, at the outset of the self-incrimination provision, the reliance on physical evidence i.e. biological analysis, handwriting, etc. did not exist. Geyh's argument contains a startling point.

> If the right is designed to assure that any evidence gathered against the accused is obtained through the exertions of the prosecution alone, it would be inappropriate for the prosecution to garner evidence against the suspect by means that compel him to assist in producing such evidence, regardless of whether that evidence takes the form of testimony or not.[22]

If the right not to be compelled to be a witness against himself but to be a witness means to convey or impart evidence, then the question is therefore begged if one provides evidence that is incriminating is one then a witness against oneself? Niceties not precluded, one cannot perform one part of the task without risking the other. The earlier state courts appeared to have the same opinion in their positions on the matter.

Further, if a suspect is advised of his rights as per Miranda, why must he be read his rights on more than one occasion or even in his entire lifetime? The rights do not change over time and, if a suspect could not remember certain portions or the entire contents of the wording, could he not then request them to be read to him again? It appears that the Warren Court created a myriad of avenues wherein a suspect could launch various appeals for his defense. Further consideration of the "activist" court will be addressed in the conclusion of this research.

The Supreme Court, although not an elected body, appears over time to feed the needs of the public and, on rare occasions, the dictates of the executive branch (Franklin D. Roosevelt in his confrontation with the Supreme Court on matters of the New Deal). This outside "will" or pressure perhaps guides the Supreme Court in its interpretation of the Constitution. The wording contained in the Constitution does not change, but new meanings are attributed to the text through the political process, either quickly and forcibly (F.D.R. in the New Deal), or over the long run by

---

[22] Ibid., p. 64.

replacing judges as they retire with judges who hold contemporary values expressed in the political make-up of the other two branches.

Gabriel Almond posits his explanation of a political culture by stating that the Anglo-American political system is both homogeneous and secular in nature. He states that "a secular political culture is multi-valued, is rational and calculating, bargaining and experimental . . . ."[23] Part and parcel of his opinion is the sharing of values between the competing viewpoints. Although different viewpoints are furthered, no one singular viewpoint is completely repressed. It is easy to agree with this position, but there are also intangibles; a feeling for fairness in the United States perhaps better described as political emotion. This political emotion blends with the resultant legal system and justifies in its proper era those fundamental Court holdings that shift toward and away from the government or suspect at various times. Were this not the case, there would be no rational explanation on how the state courts could view the Fifth Amendment in a broad favorable light in the late nineteenth and early twentieth century and, with fifty years of so deciding, bear witness to the United States Supreme Court vastly narrowing the protection granted by this amendment. Even considering the viewpoint of Wigmore and his close association with the United States Supreme Court in the early twentieth century, there were learned judges sitting on state supreme courts who rejected Wigmore's tight interpretation by issuing appellate decisions which would, fifty years later, be held to be non-viable by members of this most august body. However, over this fifty year period, the political emotion was changing towards a more liberal viewpoint on some amendments and more conservative on others. The Fourteenth Amendment was, perhaps, the most important legal vehicle to this phenomenon. In making some of these changes, evidenced by Wade and Gilbert, the Court failed to answer what the distinction may be between "compelled submission" in Schmerber and "compelled assistance" in Wade and Gilbert.

Wigmore was wrong. His assessment of testimony vis-a-vis the Fifth Amendment is in error because he disregards, for simplicity's sake, the fact that the individual may be the sole possessor of some particular evidence. To compel him to produce that essence of evidence that is housed within his own body completely

---

[23] Gabriel A. Almond, "Comparative Political Systems," *The Journal of Politics* Vol. 18. (1955):398.

ignores the "self" in self-incrimination. If the evidence is within the individual i.e. knowledge, body fluids, etc., the Fifth Amendment makes no distinction between non-physical evidence, such as verbal communication/confession, and the more physical, such as blood, hair and other bodily "knowledge" (DNA). However, to have the position prevail creates problems for the enforcement of law upon which, quite often, can hang political stability. A severe inconvenience ensues. However, if the intent is to circumvent the Bill of Rights, then the political process allows for such eventualities, but the political danger lies in the engagement of that process. It seems inconceivable that the Founding Fathers would allow for the extraction of body fluids and find repulsive the compelling of verbal confessions. Again, inconvenience to the criminal justice system looms large, but constitutional issues are found to be inconvenient when they are exercised for, at that time, their true worth as a protection is tested on the anvil of political/legal expediency.

Public Expectations of the Government

The entire Bill of Rights was predicated upon keeping government out of church, speech, one's home, etc. Is it likely they would allow government into one's veins?

So it here appears that the rights of the individual bow to this political expediency. To carry it one step further, it is plausible to envision situations where only the barring of physical torture or extreme deprivation could be the only barriers to the acquisition of information (confession) from a suspect in custody by the enforcement arm of politics, law enforcement!

> The basic purpose that lies behind the privilege against self-incrimination does not relate to protecting the innocent from conviction, but rather to preserving the integrity of a judicial system in which even the guilty are not to be convicted unless the prosecution "shoulder the entire load."[24]

Hardgrave and Bill wrote and outlined what they perceived to be the elements of our political culture. They are, in part:

A.   "specific roles or structures such as legislative bodies, executives, etc."

B.   "incumbents of roles -- monarchs, legislators, administrators"

---

[24] Tehan v. United States ex rel. Shott, 382 U.S. 406, 415 (1966)

C.   "particular public *policies*, decisions, or enforcement of decisions"[25]

The public defines itself in relation to these structures. Part of the relationship is how each person is affected by the structures in place and whether or not the population agrees with the various outcomes of governmental (criminal justice) actions. With the political culture cutting across all lines of demarcation, such as class, religion and race, and with the resultant different points of reference from the individual to the system, it is paramount that simplicity of expression of the law be utilized at all times. If interpretation of the law conflicts with the public's perception then "the balance between governmental power and responsiveness, between consensus and cleavage, between citizen influence and citizen passivity"[26] becomes questionable, unstable and problematic. Therefore, out of Wigmore's position comes only chaos brought about by the disillusionment of the public with the effectiveness of the criminal justice system to:

A.   deal with crime

B.   protect one according to the dictates of the United States Constitution

It is possible that Almond's position is valid "that people act in certain ways that can be variously categorized *because* they have internalized certain orientations of action."[27] This orientation is focused on political/legal viewpoint held by the individual. This is important to note because the average citizen is not a legal, philosophical entity, but nevertheless, that individual's perception of the law is his point of reference. If the vast majority of citizens feel the Bill of Rights is too broad in the manner in which the Supreme Court interprets it, then frustration and political depression are a political outcome with political instability a resultant destination. On the other hand, if the interpretations are too strict, the protections imagined shrink in their applicability and are viewed as near useless. Again, political depression may set in.

It could be argued that the various stances of the United States Supreme Court, by the very fact that they appear to vacillate in legal viewpoint over time, are a clear indication of reaction to the political depression of the population by the Court. This

---

[25] James A. Bill and Robert Hardgrave, *Comparative Politics: The Quest for Theory* (Columbus, OH: Charles E. Merrill Publishing Company, 1973) p. 87.
[26] Ibid. P. 91.
[27] Ibid. P. 93.

research disagrees with Philip Converse's position that, "The concept of political culture emphasizes that each individual has some sort of orientation to the political world. He does not, however, necessarily have *opinions* about it."[28] Is not one's orientation or viewpoint his own opinion of where he stands in relationship to what it is he is orienting to? One must have both simultaneously. This research has referred to this blend as political emotion.

The Use of Psychology in Interrogations

If a suspect is compelled to give some example of physical evidence, the argument could be made that, in this case, blood is possessed by the suspect. This is a truism evidencing that, indeed, the suspect does possess blood, but further in the blood is the DNA or other items of evidentiary value, and producing the blood sample need not be accompanied by any other testimony.

If one now considers the argument of "compel submission" which was not addressed by the Court in either Wade or Gilbert, another player enters the field. Where and how does one assess the point at which psychological pressure "compels" one to confess? Obviously the threshold for such a point exists, but how does the political process, through its legislative bodies, address this problem? If all psychological pressure is banned, what then will remain lawful for the admittance of a confession? Even a confession totally and freely offered has, as its foundation, some psychological basis and could thus be argued by a defense attorney possessing little legal imagination.

That psychological methods are used by many police interrogators is well understood. However, the term "psychological" conjures up, in many minds, images of prolonged and intense methods to "brainwash" the suspect into submission. It cannot be denied that, in some instances, this perhaps has occurred in the past with more frequency than in the present. Giving someone the "third degree" was *de riguer* prior to the Supreme Court decisions of the 1960's.

To be considered though are several points. First, what is it the police are attempting to do? Second, what is precisely prescribed or proscribed by law? The political climate must also be taken into account for it is at those times of extreme fear by the population that the nuances and protections guaranteed by the United

---

[28] Ibid. P. 93

States Constitution come under severe pressure to be changed or ignored. This political emotion can then make room for more liberal allowances in actual or near police misconduct in the area of interrogating suspects. What is the balance acceptable to the population in trade-offs of protection or safety vis-a-vis the surrendering of some "rights" in order to become more secure in their safety? If the population feels rather secure, then the mere "raising of the voice" by the interrogator in confronting the suspect could possibly be viewed as abusive and psychologically overpowering, thus placing the interrogator outside the bounds of acceptable behavior as it is viewed by the law. Under the more adverse situations, the opposite may very well apply.

Within the individual there are various experiences used by that person to maintain a state of homeostasis within his nervous system. Creating an imbalance in this system can bring on various degrees of depression and anxiety which the individual could find to be intolerable and he may, consequently, confess in order to remove those items from his world (interrogator and his questions) thereby allowing his nervous system to return to normal.[29] The problem created here is that the threshold of intolerance is different for all persons. How then does the legislature redefine what is acceptable? How far does the present protection offered go in its guaranties? How secure are those guaranties?

At What Risk to Remain Silent?

It is a plausible position to require that no risk, or at the very most, only minimal risk be possible by invoking a right or privilege guaranteed by the highest law in the land. Does a suspect run certain risks by adopting this position? If so, how can the State utilize this against the suspect? A variety of case law has been generated by such questions and it is necessary to examine this possible scenario to help properly evaluate what protections mean when legislated by the political system. Law is the political contract between the people and the government. The United States Constitution offers various protections to the people from the weight of the government.

---

[29] Joseph L. Kibitlewski, "The Use of Psychology in Interrogation," paper presented at the 55th annual meeting of the Mississippi Academy of Sciences, Jackson, MS., 22 February 1991.

Of early note are the cases of *Twining v. New Jersey*[30] and *Adamson v. California*.[31] In Twining, the Supreme Court stated that the "Fifth Amendment was not binding on states," therefore no protection was possible through the Fifth Amendment to cases in state courts. In Adamson, the Supreme Court allowed the state to mention that the accused refused to testify. By 1964 both the make-up of the Supreme Court and the decisions rendered by the Supreme Court had begun to change. In *Mallory v. Hogan*[32] the Supreme Court now stated that it was improper for judicial comment to be made to the jury that the accused failed to testify. However, by 1978 the pendulum again started to swing the other way. In *Lakeside v. Oregon*[33] the judge at trial advised the jury that the accused invoked his right not to testify and, because it was the right of the accused to invoke this privilege, the jury should draw no adverse inference from the accused's decision not to testify.

This whole viewpoint appears to be incongruous. We empanel a jury, allow the jury to hear what can be described as "complex" testimony and presentation of evidence and then expect a jury not to take note of the fact that the defendant did not testify. The jury is there for the sole purpose of evaluating the evidence offered and what it means. Surely it will not go unnoticed that the defendant failed to testify! Whether the judge or the prosecutor make note of that to the jury without attaching specific guilty/not guilty values to it seems trite in importance. Is it not human to wonder why someone, who professes to be innocent, not take the stand in his defense? Legal argument notwithstanding, is it not plausible -- perhaps certain -- that this thought pattern will enter the minds of many, if not all, the jurors? It should be sufficient to advise the jury as in the case of Lakeside for proper interpretation. But again, this looks questionable when viewed alongside "compelled" testimony/evidence such as required through blood sampling, etc. Other than direct admonition to consider this a guilty act on the part of the defendant not to testify, nothing more need be offered.

---

[30] Twining v. New Jersey, 211 U.S. 78, 29 S.Ct. 14, 53 L.Ed. 97 (1908).
[31] Adamson v. California, 332 U.S. 46, 67 S.Ct. 1962, 91 L.Ed. 1093 (1947).
[32] Mallory v. Hogan, 378 U.S. 1, 84 S.Ct. 1489, 12 L.Ed. 2d. 653 (1964).
[33] Lakeside v. Oregon, 435 U.S. 333, 55 L. Ed. 2d 319, 98 S. Ct. 1091 (1978).

Immunity and Self-Incrimination

The real sticking point however is the use of immunity to "compel" the suspect or witness to testify. The Fifth Amendment makes no mention of granting immunity from prosecution in exchange for testimony. It works in this fashion. First, there are two separate privileges against compulsory self-incrimination:

A. The privilege of the accused

B. The privilege of a witness

The Accused

The accused does not have to take the stand and does not have to testify. The prosecutor may not comment on the accused's failure to testify except in fair response if the accused's defense counsel mentions to the jury in closing argument that the state did not allow his client to take the stand. If the accused does elect to take the stand he/she must answer all relevant questions concerning the charge.

The Witness

The witness is cloaked with the privilege to refuse to disclose any matter that may "tend to incriminate" him. This privilege covers criminal proceedings only, not civil. If the answer to the questions merely ridicules, embarrasses or disgraces the witness, no privilege is extended unless, again, there are criminal implications.

So, we come now to the grant of "immunity" from prosecution for the witness. Two other factors also apply:

A. If the witness was acquitted of the crime and therefore cannot be re-prosecuted, the witness can be compelled to testify

B. If the statute of limitations has run its course and prosecution again is no longer a reality, the privilege does not come into play

In the first instance, the grant of immunity may be given by either the law, the prosecutor or the judge. The witness is thus compelled to testify. If the witness refuses to testify he/she can be held in contempt of court. Our legal system takes note of our Federal system in that a grant of immunity by either state or Federal proceedings carries its protection of immunity over to the other (Murphy [1964]).[34]

The use of witness immunity is further bifurcated by the types of immunity possible. There are the Transactional and the Use and Derivative Use types of

---

[34] Murphy v. Waterfront Commission, 378 U.S. 52 (1964).

immunity. The Transactional grant means that the witness can no longer be prosecuted for any occurrence stemming from the transaction. The Use and Derivative Use immunity however, is different. The witness could be prosecuted for the same charge if independent evidence, exclusive of the testimony, can be discovered. Transactional immunity is not necessary to compel testimony (Kastigar [1972]).[35] In Kastigar, the witness refused to testify under Use and Derivative Use with the point that Transactional immunity must be granted. The United States Supreme Court disagreed.

The privilege of the witness may also be waived. The waiver can take place in three ways. First, only the witness can assert his privilege. If he fails to do so when the incriminating question is asked, the privilege is waived. Second, if the witness discloses a self-incriminating fact, all further facts relating to the privilege are waived. And third, if the accused takes the stand, he or she must answer all relevant inquiries to the charge.

Although diplomatic immunity also is involved through international law, it is beyond the scope of this research (see Appendix for additional types of immunity).

The Use and Derivative Use immunity was perhaps most noted by the case of Colonel Oliver North and the congressional hearings concerning the Iran/Contra arms deal. In this governmental proceeding, we come full circle in the government's quest for knowledge from the ordeals of the pre-Magna Carta era to the present day example of Col. Oliver North.[36] This matter-of-State clearly indicates that the needs of the government are still present, but that the evolution of time along with the evolution of political thought and expression have dramatically changed how the proceedings are now carried forth.

Colonel North was granted Use and Derivative Use immunity in order to elicit information he possessed concerning the involvement of various governmental officials' and agencies' actions circumventing Congressional dictates regarding the supply of arms to the Contras. After securing immunity, Colonel North implicated himself in actions that were clearly in violation of the law. At the conclusion of the Congressional hearings, Colonel Oliver North was prosecuted for his illegal involvements. He was convicted on three of the twelve counts and he appealed. His

---

[35] Kastigar v. United States, 406 U.S. 441 (1972).
[36] United States v. Oliver North, 910 F.2d 843 (D.C. Cir).

appeal centered on the point that some of the evidence used by the special prosecutor and witnesses had genesis from his testimony during the Congressional proceedings and should have been suppressed. In a two to one decision, the United States Court of Appeals agreed ruling that the preceding judge must determine "witness-by witness; if necessary line-by-line and item-by-item" if the special prosecutor or any of the witnesses in Colonel North's trial were influenced by his testimony at the Congressional hearings under which he was granted his immunity. The Government/special prosecutor found this to be too cumbersome in burden to cope with and subsequently elected not to retry Colonel North.

Controversy surrounding the "right to silence" is as unsettled today as it has been these past four centuries. Amar and Lettow[37] indicate, by their position, to once and for all clearly outline what is protected and what is not. If *Counselman v. Hitchcock*[38] did not accomplish this feat, then *Kastigar v. United States* surely muddied the waters. Whereas in Counselman the Supreme Court indicated that compelled testimony carried all use of the obtained information involved in subsequent criminal proceedings, Kastigar said that some use of the compelled testimony can be used. Amar and Lettow would so structure the use of immunity as to completely strip the protection to near meaningless guidelines. Their proposal would allow for testimony to be compelled with the proviso that the compelled testimony never be introduced over the defendant's objection in a criminal trial. The point being that the defendant then is not a witness against himself in a "criminal case," but the fruits of these compelled pretrial words will generally be admissible."[39] This research finds Amar and Lettow very disturbing to say the least. The focus of their research appears to be to assist the courts because, under the present interpretations of the protection, the "courts cripple innocent defendants while the guilty wrap themselves in the clause and walk free."[40] If so, then how do the "guilty" go free? The pretrial civilized hearing proposed by Amar and Lettow would be

---

[37] Akhil Reed Amar and Renee B. Lettow, "Fifth Amendment First Principles: The Self-Incrimination Clause" *Michigan Law Review* Vol. 93, No. 5 (March 1995):857-928.

[38] Counselman v. Hitchcock, 142 U.S. 547 (1892).

[39] Akhil Reed Amar and Renee B. Lettow, "Fifth Amendment First Principles: The Self-Incrimination Clause" *Michigan Law Review* Vol. 93, No. 5 (March 1995):859.

[40] Ibid. p. 861.

presided over by a magistrate or judge for the purpose of eliciting testimony that the suspect must give truthfully.

It is difficult on the one hand to realize that the privilege against self-incrimination was not sooner in place in police interrogations. Early legal reasoning embodied that compulsion to testify meant *legal* compulsion. With the suspect being neither threatened with perjury nor contempt for failing to testify at all, it could not be said that he was being "compelled" during the police interrogation to be a witness against himself and therefore, contrary to the privilege extended. "As the police have no legal right to make the suspect answer, there is no legal obligation to answer to which a privilege in the technical sense can apply."[41]

Introduction at trial of additional facts obtained through scientific methods presents philosophical as well as legal debate. Voice stress analysis and polygraphs each offer technical assistance to determine truth. In order to be admitted at trial, the method used must first comply with the "Frye"[42] requirements. This essentially lays the groundwork for acceptance of the method used, if that method is generally accepted within its own scientific community and given that certain guidelines are followed. It is in this manner that blood typing evidence determination is allowed as a valid method of determining blood type from various types of body fluid samples.

The research would be remiss in its mission if other predictable possibilities were not considered under the penumbra of the various collateral issues yet to be addressed by the Fifth Amendment. The United States has a legal history of stretching and condensing protections offered by the Bill of Rights. With the First Amendment, Supreme Court decisions have broadened the "freedom of speech" clause to include nudity and flag burning as expressions of free speech. Surely if speech is verbal, then non-verbal communication is also considered speech. Yet in matters important to the Fifth Amendment, non-verbal (communication) is considered outside the realm of speech and not protected. Of significant nature

---

[41] Yale Kamisar, Wayne R. LaFave, and Jerold H. Israel, *Modern Criminal Procedure: Cases, Comments and Questions* 7th ed. (St. Paul, MN: West Publishing Co., 1990), p. 440.

[42] Frye v. United States, 293 Fed. 1013 (App. D.C.) (1923)
". . . while courts will go a long way in admitting expert testimony deduced from a well-recognized scientific principle or discovery, the thing from which the deduction is made must be sufficiently established to have gained general acceptance in the particular field in which it belongs."

comes the following question. Who may be given immunity to testify? To fully appreciate this question we must outline the problem again through legal case history.

Multiple Personalities and
Self-Incrimination

If one can be given immunity in order for a court to secure testimony against the individual or another, can the court grant immunity to one "personality" who dwells within a singular body with other personalities? On the surface, the concept at first appears absurd. Under examination with case history, serious questions come into focus. This disorder is manifested by the existence within a single person of several distinct personalities or personality states. The *Diagnostic and Statistical Manual for Mental Disorders* describes personality thusly: "Personality is here defined as a relatively enduring pattern of perceiving, relating to, and thinking about the environment and one's self that is exhibited in a wide range of important social and personal contexts."[43] The Manual goes on to illustrate how in classic cases there are at least two fully developed personalities, or, there can exist one distinct personality and one or more personality states. It is possible for each personality to have unique memories, behavior patterns and social relationships. In the adult population the number of personalities or personality states can number over one hundred. The Manual also states that in such cases about fifty percent have fewer than ten personalities and, of course, the other fifty percent shows more than ten personalities. What is important is the realization that at some point in time the person's behavior is under the control of two or more of these personalities. This change of personality is sudden in nature, although there have been known cases where the changeover has been gradual. Whether the personalities are known to each other or not also occurs on a case-by-case basis. In some instances one personality is in conflict with one or more of the other resident personalities. In many cases, the existence of other personalities can be quite unknown to the one personality until treatment is sought for some psychological condition. There are other distinct points that also bear mentioning. One personality may adapt quite well, be gainfully employed, while a separate personality could be clearly dysfunctional. There are studies that show different physiological traits between personalities as well as

---

[43] American Psychiatric Association, *Diagnostic and Statistical Manual of Mental Disorders*, 3rd ed. rev. (Washington D.C.: American Psychiatric Association, 1987), p. 269.

different I.Q., different responses to the same medication, even to each having different eyeglass prescriptions. It is not unusual for a different sex, race or age to be the position of each personality; behaving appropriately according to the sex or age so posited.

These are a few of the considerations that the law must attempt to address. In attempting to be fair, the law appears to be entering a new legal quagmire. In the case of *State v. Halcomb*[44] the defendant confessed and ultimately was convicted. The personality that confessed was also the personality that committed the crime. The confession and charges were both disputed by the "principal"(?) personality. The appeal of the conviction was denied and the conviction was affirmed. In *Arizona v. Carlson*[45] the preliminary hearing witnessed three of James Carlson's personalities, each being placed under oath separately! If the judge saw fit to place each personality under oath, is then the court treating each as a separate legal entity? This brings the question, if one personality is guilty, the others must be innocent unless a conspiracy can be established. Should an innocent personality suffer the consequences of a guilty person?

Miranda and Its Effects

What has been the effect of Miranda upon the actions of the police? Were there any social costs? Both questions were researched by Paul Cassell individually.

The first study addressed is titled "Police Interrogation in the 1990's: An Empirical Study of the Effects of Miranda," conducted by Paul G. Cassell and Bret S. Hayman. The focus of their study was to determine if, as the Supreme Court has ruled, Miranda is "prophylactic," what would a cost/benefit analysis determine? Is the effectiveness of police interrogations eroded by Miranda? If this is weighed against the suspect's rights, is there balance in the law? The sample used was obtained in Salt Lake County, Utah and encompassed a sample of more than two hundred cases. The study examined:

A. Frequency of waivers

B. Police compliance with Miranda

C. Role confessions played in prosecutions

Basic findings produced the following data:

---

[44] State v. Halcomb, 3 NCA 169, 1993 NEB. App. Lexis 185.
[45] *The Times,* Thursday, January 6, 1994.

A.   21 percent of all suspects were never questioned

B.   16 percent of suspects invoked their Miranda rights

C.   only about 33 percent gave confessions

The research pointed out that the 33 percent figure is lower than pre-Miranda onset by the Supreme Court. When compared to other countries that do not have Miranda warnings, this same 33 percent was again lower indicating that perhaps Miranda has depressed confession rates.

The comparison with rates of confessions in other countries is a valid one considering that the law in other countries was a part of the basis for consideration of the Warren Court, which issued Miranda. Chief Justice Warren's opinion issued in Miranda stated that foreign jurisdictions followed comparable rules with no ill effects. Cassell goes on to illustrate that, "British confession rates fell from over 60percent before 1986 to between 40 and 50percent when the Miranda-style Police and Criminal Act was imposed in that year."[46]

Another datum which bears consideration in Cassell's paper is Table 2.

TABLE 2

QUESTIONING RESULT BY LENGTH OF QUESTIONING
(N=173; 87 unavailable)

Length of Questioning	Questioning Successful		Questioning Unsuccessful		Total	
	No.	%	No.	%	No.	%
≤ 5 Minutes	6	33.3%	12	66.7%	18	100.0%
6-10 Minutes	11	40.7%	16	59.3%	27	100.0%
11-15 Minutes	5	62.5%	3	37.5%	8	100.0%
16-30 Minutes	15	68.2%	7	31.8%	22	100.0%
31-60 Minutes	4	40.0%	6	60.0%	10	100.0%
60+ Minutes	1	100.0%	0	0.0%	1	100.0%
Total	42	48.8%	44	51.2%	86	100.0%

Source: Paul G. Cassell and Bret S. Hayman. "Police Interrogation in the 1990s: An Empirical Study of the Effects of Miranda," 43 *UCLA Law Review* 001 (1996):59.

---

[46] Paul G. Cassell and Bret S. Hayman. "Police Interrogation in the 1990s: An Empirical Study of the Effects of Miranda," 43 *UCLA Law Review* 001 (1996):42.

This table clearly shows that interrogation by police need not be unduly long in duration to obtain a confession. This table illustrates the progression of success as the length of time interrogating a suspect increases from 5 minutes to 60 minutes. This clearly is not up to Star Chamber standards! This research supports the position that interrogations are not extended periods of time in which the suspect is held incommunicado. Further, the collected data showed that most interrogations were held during the daytime hours. These data were important because the protection to remain silent was intended, in the first instance, to prevent the accused from torture. With this in mind, this research dealt earlier with torture, perceived and actual. From Cassell's paper, table 3 shows the interrogation to be more successful when the accused is confronted with evidence against him. The stronger the evidence, the more likely that a confession will occur.

TABLE 3

QUESTIONING RESULT BY STRENGTH OF EVIDENCE
(N=173; 30 unavailable)

Strength of Evidence	Invoked Rights		Questioning Successful		Questioning Unsuccessful		Total	
	No.	%	No.	%	No.	%	No.	%
Overwhelming	3	33.3%	5	55.6%	1	11.1%	9.0	100.0%
Strong	12	16.7%	34	47.2%	26	36.1%	72	100.0%
Moderate	4	9.3%	18	41.9%	21	48.8%	43	100.0%
Weak	0	0.0%	5	26.3%	14	73.7%	19	100.0%
Total	19	13.3%	62	43.4%	62	43.4%	14	100.0%

Source: Paul G. Cassell and Bret S. Hayman. "Police Interrogation in the 1990s: An Empirical study of the Effects of Miranda," 43 *UCLA Law Review* 001 (1996):62.

Cassell goes on to demonstrate that the Supreme Court's "prophylactic Miranda doctrine sweeps more broadly than the Fifth Amendment and is over broad in that its application excludes some statements made during custodial interrogations that are, in fact, not coercive."[47] Cassell's position is well taken that ". . . a suspect has no

---

[47] New York v. Quarles, 467 U.S. 649, 684 n. 7 (1984). (Marshall, J. dissenting).

legitimate interest under the Constitution in avoiding confessing; rather, a suspect is entitled to be free from unconstitutional coercion."[48] If "coercion" is the proscribed element, then we must look to Chief Justice White's position. Chief Justice White finds it difficult to agree with the contention that if "the police ask a single question 'Do you have anything to say?' such a query becomes coercive."[49] Should Miranda be required to ask the simple question? In Moran[50] the Court "now tells us that Miranda is 'a carefully crafted balance designed to fully protect both the defendants' and society's interest.'"[51] These statements by the Court are without empirical data to support them and, on the face of it, it appears that society pays more than its share of the balancing act. Clearly the score is "advantage" suspect.

With society's interest now the point, the second portion of Cassell's research[52] gains prominence. The methodology used in this study did not focus on confession suppression rates, but attempted to delineate the number of confessions "lost" or not obtained because of Miranda. The studies were two-sided. One study looked at the numbers on a "before" and "after" Miranda onset. The second looked at the confession rate in the United States vis-a-vis other countries that use different methods to direct police interrogations.

Before and After Studies

As table 4 shows, there were drops in the confession rate in all cities with the exception of Los Angeles. Data from Los Angeles was contaminated because of variance in the questions asked. The studies in Los Angeles are known as the Dorado[53] studies. These studies are discredited on two points. First, many replies were incomplete or inconsistent. Second, a follow-up re-designed questionnaire included in the analysis "confessions and admissions" or other statements. Also, Dorado was compared in Los Angeles a few weeks after Miranda and may have included pre-Miranda data.

---

[48] Paul G. Cassell and Bret S. Hayman. "Police Interrogation in the 1990s: An Empirical Study of the effects of Miranda," 43 *UCLA Law Review* 001 (1996):94.

[49] Ibid.

[50] Moran v. Burbine, 475 U.S. 412, 433 n. 4 (1986).

[51] Paul G. Cassell and Bret S. Hayman. "Police Interrogation in the 1990s: An Empirical Study of the Effects of Miranda,," 43 *UCLA Law Review* 001 (1996):96.

[52] Paul G. Cassell. "Miranda's Social Cost: An Empirical Reassessment," *Northwestern University Law Review* Vol. 90, No. 2 (1996).

[53] People v. Dorado, 398 P. 2d (Cal.) (en Banc), Cert. denied, 381 U.S. 937 (1965).

TABLE 4

ESTIMATES OF CHANGES IN THE CONFESSION
RATE DUE TO MIRANDA

City	Confession Rate Before	Confession Rate After	Change	Major Problems?
Pittsburgh	48.5%	29.9%	-18.6%	
N.Y. County	49.0%	14.5%	-34.5%	
Philadelphia	45% (est./der.)	20.4% (der.)	-24.6%	
"Seaside City"	68.9%	66.9%	-2.0%	?
New Haven-1960-66	58-63% (est.)	48.2%	-10.15%	Yes
New Haven-calculated	?	?	-16.0%	
D.C.	21.5% (der.)	20.0% (der.)	-1.5%	Yes
Kansas City	?	?	-6% (der.)	?
Kings County	45% (est./der.)	29.5% (der.)	-15.5%	
New Orleans	40% (est.)	28.2%	-11.8%	?
Chicago homicides	53% (der.)	26.5% (der.)	-26.5%	?
Los Angeles	40.4%	50.2%	+9.8%	Yes
Average of Studies Without Major Problems			16.1%	

Source: Paul G. Cassell. "Miranda's Social Cost: An Empirical Reassessment,"
Northwestern University Law Review Vol. 90, No. 2 (1996): 416.

est. - estimated
der. = derived

"Thus the study is not really a before and after study, but rather an after-after study."[54]
It is Cassell's contention, based upon the analysis shown in the "before" and "after"
Table 4, that "the best estimate is that Miranda results in a lost confession in roughly
one out of every six criminal cases in this country."[55]

In summary, this chapter has provided a comprehensive overview of the legal
and political processes which culminated in the present provisions of Miranda. This
moreover shows that this process is still dynamic and, to further underscore this
comment, there is the realization that when Miranda was decided by the Supreme

---

[54] Paul G. Cassell. "Miranda's Social Cost: An Empirical Reassessment," *Northwestern University Law Review* Vol. 90, No. 2 (1996):416.
[55] Ibid. p. 417.

Court, its margin of inception was by one vote. The Supreme Court has witnessed its periodic intrusion upon the states' legal viewpoint of confessions and has, on occasion, in its estimation, found the states' position to be legally wanting.

Of additional consideration is the political implication of providing to the public a vantage point to help reaffirm its belief in the abstract quality of the law through its political process. The period of Miranda was one of turmoil within the society on many levels. The Government was involved in attempting to justify its military decisions regarding Viet Nam; the civil rights issues of the South were producing clashes between state and Federal authorities; environmental issues as well as sex-based employment problems were all vying for the Government's attention on behalf of some portion of society. Issues of the marches, riots and other expressions of political discontent required, perhaps, some expression by an authoritative governing body to provide reassurance to the public that the Government was not abandoning it to a dictatorial process. The rulings of the Supreme Court may have performed a function of political salvation by instituting restraints upon the most visible expression of the Government -- the criminal justice system. It is not the position of this research that the Supreme Court acted under these concerns, but rather, that the end product was serendipitous to the era.

The public, through the decisions of the Supreme Court, now had cause to believe that the protections of the Bill of Rights were indeed real in their application. Miranda gave way to all types of legal challenges. Areas of immunity, violations of the right to remain silent, even those concerned with the peculiar psychological malady of "multiple personalities," were all given their opportunity in this ever-changing legal quagmire.

CHAPTER 5
ENGLISH LAW AND SUSPECTS' RIGHTS

A direct comparison of English case law and United States case law was made difficult because the variations on a legal theme, so prevalent in the judicial system of the United States, were found to be lacking in its English counterpart. The cases selected for comparison from the English records were chosen because they most closely addressed those issues concerned with the research. The interplay between English civil and criminal law had to likewise be examined, as some issues of protection of the right to silence were shown to be challenged in their effectiveness when considerations of law that existed between the civil and criminal proceedings of an accused were taken into account.

The research found, as a by-product, that some areas of recent concern in the United States courts are not at all present in the English courts. Most notable is the recent plethora of cases in the United States with the accused claiming to contain multiple personalities. There is little evidence that the mental health professionals in England consider this as a valid malady and, therefore, it is not unusual to find it missing from legal proceedings. The massive change of Federal law into the provinces of the state courts in the United States is also lacking within the English system, as England does not possess a federal type of political division. The struggle, therefore, to reconcile Federal law with state law does not present itself in England. Curiously, also missing is the formation of "judicial rules," witnessed in the United States legal system by virtue of the Supreme Court edicts. Such judicial rules as the "Miranda rule," or the "exclusionary rule," of the United States type, are not within the province of authority of English appellate judges.

Of concern in the area of English law and suspects' rights, with considerable possibility of strong impact, was the amount and motivation for Parliament to have overturned its own laws in respect to the problem under consideration. With the availability of quick judicial viewpoint modification of Parliament vis-a-vis changing the viewpoint of the United States Supreme Court through its limitations placed on replacement of those seated on the court, we examined if this availability for swiftness was motivated to benefit the suspect and if so, what were the conditions that brought it about.

With the English system, Parliament can be brought down in a matter of days and replaced within a matter of weeks, thereby possibly changing the political thought behind the provided judicial review. In the United States, this process could conceivably be stretched over a twenty-year period or even longer. How then has this been a factor, if at all?

"Miranda" - English Style

Although England is the birthplace of the individual's "right to silence", it is here that we find changes, however slight, occurring. At the heart of the matter is the wording of the new warning -- Miranda, if you will -- that has been codified into the legal system. This warning, given by the police to a suspect, used to be "You do not have to say anything unless you wish to do so, but what you say may be given in evidence." This caution has been replaced by the following: "You do not have to say anything. But if you do not mention now something which you later use in your defence, the court may decide that your failure to mention it now strengthens the case against you. A record will be made of anything you say and it may be given in evidence if you are brought to trial." The controversy over this change in the wording of the caution will be addressed further in the succeeding chapter.

Of comparison interest is the area requiring the suspect to provide certain types of exemplars for evidentiary purposes. In England, the suspect may refuse and this refusal, the research shows, can have an adverse impact on the suspect when the refusal is coupled with additional evidence to help convict the suspect. Adverse as this may appear, the fact that the suspect does exercise the right not to provide evidence is in keeping with both the letter of the law and its spirit. "Cautions" must be administered if the person is suspect of an offense before any questions are put to him to obtain information. No "caution" is needed to establish identity, establish ownership or to search the person. As soon as the officer questioning the person believes that he should be prosecuted and has a good chance to convict, the officer will ask the person if he has anything to say. When a person is charged for multiple offenses, the person will be "cautioned" for all charges. When the person is charged or informed he may be charged, he will be "cautioned."

As stated earlier in the research, a direct comparison in all instances may not be possible given the nuances of the law under each political system. The research discussed at some length how information obtained under one type of legal setting could be used in another proceeding if, under United States law, there were Fifth Amendment issues controlling. In England we find a similar situation with quite a different outcome than what would be expected in the United States.

Civil and Criminal Law

The research has shown that there is a division of the law in the United States, not only between cases of civil or criminal origin, but also between legal systems i.e. state or Federal jurisdiction. The English system benefits, or suffers, from a division of law into only civil or criminal courts. These differences will be further addressed in the succeeding chapter. It is mentioned here so that inclusion of both civil and criminal cases, under English law, may provide a clearer understanding of the rights and protection in question.

The research of English law records revealed substantial insight into areas of law both of a criminal and civil nature. Whereas the court in either division may order or request certain "intimate samples" of evidence for comparison purposes, their actual presence may not be forthcoming. The failure to produce these "samples" does impact upon the accused, but in different ways than under the law in the United States.

The case of *R. v. Tottenham Justices Ex Parte ML Queens Bench* deals with the prosecution being able to obtain "edge" prints of the palm of a juvenile suspect in a burglary under investigation. Argument by the defense did not center upon the point that this was prevented by law because it would be providing "self" evidence but rather upon the proviso that perhaps "edge" prints of the palm were not themselves "palm prints" as dictated by Parliament. The prints were taken and, after conviction, an appeal was filed from which dicta for this research is reflected. The appeal was denied under two points. One, the judges agreed that the edge of the palm was a palm print in all respects and, second, "non-intimate" samples may be taken of a suspect by court order. The appeal at no time proffered the argument of providing evidence contrary to the right to remain silent. This is a clear indication of the lack of interest by English barristers to bring into prominence legal nuances for debate or consideration at the appellate level.

The case of *R. v. Brody*[1] does however hinge on the right to silence. The law being addressed in this case concerned statements made by the accused in *voire dire*. This *voire dire* under English law differs in that it more closely resembles a preliminary hearing in the United States rather than the *voir dire* in the United States which concerns itself with the jury selection process. Under English law, the accused has the right to give evidence at *voire dire* without affecting his right to remain silent at the substantive trial which is absolute and not to be made conditional by judicial discretion.[2] At the substantive trial for this case, the prosecution called as a witness the court reporter to read the notes from the *voire dire* regarding the suspect's admission that he was a member of the IRA. The defense objected but the trial judge allowed the court reporter to be heard. After a conviction on only one count out of forty-nine charges, the suspect appealed his conviction on count 49, the one which addressed his involvement as a member of the IRA. A court of appeals in Northern Ireland found for the defendant and the Crown subsequently appealed the appeal. The Crown lost its argument because of the following opinion. If the evidence at *voire dire* is relevant to the case it cannot be used against the accused at substantive trial. Further, if this evidence could be used at substantive trial it would limit the accused's freedom at *voire dire* to examine points of law contested by the defense. In this case, the *voire dire* was used to determine if the statements made by the accused at various times while in police custody were freely given or coerced. The judge at *voire dire* decided the statements made by the accused to the police might have been coerced and so the judge, at *voire dire*, disallowed statements/confessions at the substantive trial.

If the accused wants to have a determination to decide whether evidence was obtained properly by the police, he must be allowed the freedom to speak at *voire dire* without jeopardy for he cannot provide an adequate argument without giving evidence, and if his evidence were admissible at the substantive trial, the accused would suffer significant impairment of his right to silence at the trial itself. It may be reasoned that in the situation of *voire dire*, the accused is "compelled" to give evidence; this in stark contrast to the right to remain silent. ". . . no man is to be

---

[1] R. v. Brody House of Lords [1982] AC 476, [1981] All ER 705, [1983] 3 WLR 103, 73 Cr App Rep 287, 145.

[2] Wong Kam-ming v. The Queen [1979] 1 All ER at 946-947.

compelled to incriminate himself; *nemo tenetur se ipsum prodere.*"[3] The word "compelled" in that context includes being put under pressure to give evidence at *voire dire.* The appeals judge's decision in part reads:

> Any civilised system of criminal jurisprudence must accord to the judiciary some means of excluding confessions . . . the accused not to be subjected to ill treatment . . . it is therefore necessary the accused should feel free, either by his own testimony or other means, to challenge the voluntary character of the tendered statement.

It was the position of this appeals court that this right is absolute and cannot be made conditional by judicial discretion. Under the law in the United States, this type of hearing, usually held prior to trial, also precludes the use of testimony obtained at the hearing to be used at trial.

Non-Testimonial Self-Incrimination

Whereas in Brody the accused's right to silence was absolute, there are areas which allow the accused to place himself in jeopardy to various degrees by not providing evidence, to wit, "intimate samples," blood, etc. The case of *McVeigh v. Beattie*[4] is of particular interest in this regard. Although this case is civil in nature, the law is the same regarding court orders for obtaining "intimate samples." This case involved one of paternity determination brought about by a nanny employed by the defendant. The plaintiff stated that the accused had sexual intercourse upon her body and against her will and that, as a result of this unwanted sexual assault, she became pregnant. She also stated that prior to the assault she had been a virgin and had no previous sexual contact with anyone. The birth of her illegitimate child ensued. The plaintiff brought charges against the accused. The judges made a direction, under section 20 of the Family Law Act 1969, for blood tests of the parties and the child. The accused did not comply with the court direction to provide blood samples. To place the points at issue in this case, it will help to examine a companion criminal case to assist in understanding the point of demarcation between the suspect's right to remain silent and the obligation to provide "intimate samples" for the determination of fact-finding. *Reg. v. Smith*[5] is such a case for inclusion here.

---

[3] R. v. Sang [1979] 2 All ER 1222 at 1246, [1980] Ac 402 at 455 per Lord Scarman.
[4] McVeigh v. Beattie [1988] Fam 69, [1988] 2 All ER 500, [1988] 2 WLR 992, [1988] 2 FLR 67, [1988] Fam Law 290.
[5] Reg v. Smith (Robert William) [1985] 81 Cr App R 286.

Smith was charged with robbery and a search of the crime scene produced hair samples. The accused refused court direction to provide samples for comparison. Smith did not take the stand at trial and the only evidence against him was from an accomplice who implicated Smith. The jury was warned of the danger of convicting the suspect on the "uncorroborated" evidence of the accomplice, and the judge defined corroboration and directed the jury that Smith's refusal to provide hair samples was capable of amounting to corroboration. The appellate court considered the defense's position that the trial judge's direction perhaps conflicted with the basic principle that no-one was obliged to incriminate himself, and an analogy was drawn with the right to remain silent. The court of appeal held that the trial judge's direction was properly given. The appellate court found no connection between the basic right to remain silent and the producing of hair exemplars for comparison.

Reg. v. Smith was the precursor to the Police and Criminal Evidence Act 1984. In this Act, Section 62 deals with "intimate samples" which may be taken from a person in police detention, including blood samples. Several points are now important if the suspect refuses to provide these samples:

A.   Was there good cause to refuse

B.   Whether the accused be so charged for trial

C.   The court or jury, in determining guilt or innocence, i.e.,

". . . may draw such inferences from the refusal as appear proper; and the refusal may, on the basis of such inferences, be treated as, or as capable of amounting to, corroboration of any evidence against the person in relation to which the refusal is material."

These same provisions are found in sections 20 and 23 of the Family Law Reform Act 1969. The McVeigh case is almost identical with minor exceptions. The McVeigh case was civil and the samples involved were blood samples. McVeigh refused to honor the court direction to provide samples for comparison; he did, however, take the stand and denied any involvement with the plaintiff. The situation was now his word against hers. Corroboration for the plaintiff was needed. The justices hearing his case made the following determinations:

A.   McVeigh did not comply with the direction to provide blood samples.

B.   The justices treated this failure to comply as the sole evidence providing corroboration for the plaintiff's case;

hence the point of law being "On the hearing of a complaint under section 1 of this Act, the court may adjudge the defendant to be the putative father of the child but shall not do so, in a case where evidence is given by the mother, unless her evidence is corroborated in some material particular by other evidence to the court's satisfaction." In this case, the court drew an adverse inference of McVeigh's failure to comply and that failure was capable of corroborating the plaintiff's allegation that McVeigh was the father of her child.

Because of the similarity of these cases, despite definite lines of differences, a clear picture is formed as to how English law allows for evidence of this nature to be treated by the courts -- the right to remain silent notwithstanding!

Under English law, when is an interview not an interview? In *R. v. Williams*[6] the accused was in custody for one offense and had a solicitor assigned to him to advise him. While in custody for the original charge, police officers dropped by his cell for a "social visit." A few minutes after the "social visit" the accused signed a statement saying he wished to be "interviewed" by the police without the presence of his solicitor. There are in place certain safeguards for the accused. The Codes of Practice under the Police and Criminal Evidence Act 1984 offer that the accused's solicitor should be present also, that the recorded interview not be preceded by an unrecorded interview, and that a signed statement from the accused outlining his desire to see the investigating officer be obtained. Although the appellate judge found the "social visit" to be suspicious with the taped interview immediately following the visit which produced admissions on the part of the accused, the judge stated ". . . that it was the accused who wished to see the investigators, that it was he who was wanting to do a deal himself and offer assistance, and so volunteer this information . . . did not mean that the evidence should be ruled out." Further finding stated that if the suspect wishes to make a statement and if he is properly cautioned (Mirandized) the officers are not debarred from recording what the suspect has to say, after proper caution. In addition, the court ruled that the "social visit" was not an interview as defined by *R. v. Absolam,*[7] ". . . namely a series of questions directed by the police to a suspect with a view to obtaining admissions on which proceedings could be founded."

---

[6] R. v. Williams (Mark Alexander) Court of Appeal (Criminal Division) 156 JP 776.

[7] R. v. Absolam [1989] 88 Cr. App. R 336.

This case is similar to its United States' companion cases of *Michigan v. Mosely* (1975)[8] and *Oregon v. Bradshaw* (1983)[9] wherein the suspects were interrogated (United States' definition) after being Mirandized (cautioned, English definition), and attorneys having been assigned to the respective suspects. The police later re-Mirandized the suspects about an unrelated charge and obtained a confession. The United States Supreme Court held the incriminating statements in both cases to be admissible in court.

In *R. v. Kelt,*[10] the suspect argued against providing a blood sample for one investigation but did agree to provide a blood sample for another investigation. The sample was used by the police for comparison in both crimes. There was a match of the sample for the crime in which the accused refused to provide a sample, while the other crime was still under investigation. Kelt argued the police should not have used the blood sample for additional inquiries. What is of note here is that the suspect hinged his appeal on the improper extension of comparison rather than the right to silence cum right not to be compelled to provide evidence points of law.

One such case, using the argument that being "compelled" to provide evidence was contrary to the protection granted by the right to remain silent was the case of *Rank Film Distributors, Ltd. and others v. Video Information Centre and others.*[11] The plaintiffs filed suit in civil court and requested discovery with an Anton Piller order which required defendants to allow representatives of the plaintiff to enter the premises of the defendant for the purpose of looking for and removing any unauthorized films. The defendants were charged with pirating video films, making duplicate masters, duplication of the films and their subsequent distribution and sale. The defendants appealed to have the order "varied claiming if all the information was disclosed they would incriminate themselves and open themselves to criminal prosecution under the Copyright Act of 1956 s 21."[12] The plaintiffs argued that the court had the discretionary power to uphold the order and to limit its use only to the civil proceedings -- the court disagreed. The judges stated variously that the current

---

[8] Michigan v. Mosely, 423 U.S. 96, 96 S. Ct. 321, 46 L. Ed. 2d 313 (1975).

[9] Oregon v. Bradshaw, 459 U.S. 966, 103 S. Ct. 292, 74 L. Ed. 2d. 276, 51 L.W. 4940 (1983).

[10] R. v. Kelt, Court of Appeal (Criminal Division) [1994] 2 All E.R. 780.

[11] Rank Film Distributors, Ltd. and others v. Video Information Centre and others. Court of Appeal (Civil Division) [1982] AC 380, [1980] 2 All E.R. 273, [1980] 3 WLR 487, [1970] FSR 242.

[12] Ibid.

law was lacking and that legislation was needed to allow an owner his just rights to the protection of his property and a removal of the rights of self-incrimination to the extent that use of this information in criminal proceedings would be precluded. Part of the paradox was that the more criminal their activities can be made to appear, the less effective is the civil remedy that can be granted but, *prima facie*, is what the privilege achieves. Another point considered by the court was that although a subsequent criminal trial may ensue, the trial judge at that trial could refuse to allow information of a self-incriminating nature obtained through discovery at a civil trial. This argument was rejected on the grounds that this would substitute, for a privilege, a dependence on the criminal courts discretion much to the detriment of the defendant. Further, even if the direct information was excluded, the process itself could set into motion a chain of events leading to discovery of other real evidence of an incriminating nature.

Lord Wilberforce summed it up for the court thusly: "All that this House can do is to decide that the privilege against self-incrimination is capable of being involved." Here again we find the problem that the Court, civil or criminal can "compel intimate samples" but not necessarily physical items. If the Anton Piller Order in civil court can be denied upon these grounds, where the danger to the defendant is less than in criminal proceedings, it would appear the privilege against self-incrimination is eroded crossing the legal bridge from civil to criminal proceedings.

The case of *Reg - W (A minor)* Court of Appeal (Civil Division)[13] brings out yet another facet of the defendant refusing to provide blood samples in a paternity suit. In the United States civil court system, if a party to the suit is directed to produce something and its production is refused, the judge may order that person to be in contempt of court and could assess jail time until such items are produced. In England, the judge can draw any inference he wants from the failure of the defendant to provide blood samples. In this case, the judge decided that the defendant, by virtue of refusing to provide blood samples, was the father of the child. Case dicta reads in part, "By refusing to take the tests, the court believes that he is the father of A. He has chosen to reject the opportunity to prove he is not the father." It would appear

---

[13] Reg - W (A minor) Court of Appeal (Civil Division)

that this direction of the court reverted the English law back to trials of an inquisition nature wherein the accused must answer all questions and prove his own innocence!

Multiple Personality Disorder

The research was unable to discover any court cases addressing the issue of Multiple Personality Disorder and the right to silence. In fact, there do not appear to be ANY cases dealing with this phenomenon. Whether this is so because the argument is not acceptable under English law or whether the mental health professionals have not made the jump from medical to legal issues is not known. More research in the area is indicated.

Immunity and English Law

In the previous chapter, the research examined the various types of immunity that may be granted to accused persons or witnesses to obtain information in furthering investigations of various types. The various types of immunity possible under the legal code in the United States do not appear to have the same parallels under the English legal system. However, the legal database of Lexis was able to produce several instances for comparison purposes. They appeared to be concerned with civil matters with possible after-effects concluding in criminal courts. Although the case presented here in the research, Rank Film Distributors, Ltd. and others, was selected for presentation, it was not the landmark decision in such matters. The landmark case was Sociedade Nacional de Combustiveis de Angola UEE and others.[14] This case was not selected for presentation in this research because of the extensive nature of the parties involved in transnational business dealings. However, the essence of the case was very similar in the legal points argued in Rank, and, Rank being less complex in nature, it was selected for issues of both clarity and brevity. Other cases reviewed by the research also were not utilized because all were of a similar legal nature and would not add any considerable knowledge to assist with the issue at hand (see note).[15]

---

[14] Sociedade Nacional de Combustiveis de Angola UEE and others v. Lundquist and others. Court of Appeal (Civil Division) [1991] 2 QB 310, [1990] 3 All ER 283, [1991] 2 WLR 280.
[15] Cases reviewed:
R. v. Stipendiary Magistrates Ex Parte Director of the Serious Fraud Office. Queens Bench Division. Johnstone & Others v. United Norwest Co-operatives Ltd. Court of Appeal (Civil Division).

The "New" Caution

Crime does not mire itself in tradition from a by-gone era. Criminal defenses are modernized along political, economic, social and legal lines. Whereas statutes are updated, much of the basic language is founded in ideas and ideals centuries old. The wording of the new warning to replace the "caution" has elicited strong opposition from various quarters. It is unclear at first whether this opposition is guided by the fear of real "rights" erosion, or just the fact that some people are more comfortable with the well-worn, old shoes of tradition. The old warning is "You do not have to say anything unless you wish to do so, but what you say must be given in evidence." This statement is very straightforward and outlines two things. First, that you can remain silent. Second, what you say may be used in court. This is what it says. What it does not outline are the implications of remaining silent and, there are implications. Would not the unsuspecting accused be better informed if he were advised that there are possible consequences to face if he remains silent? Many of the arguments we see in opposition to this new warning place great concern on protecting the suspect, and an examination of these concerns is part of the research. Quoting Helena Kennedy, QC: "It's about an erosion of the presumption of innocence. It's an emblem of how we have stopped caring about liberty. The 'right of silence' was to protect the vulnerable and the innocent."[16] Is this comment fair? The new warning says the following: "You do not have to say anything. But, if you do not mention now something which you later use in your defence, the court may decide that your failure to mention it now strengthens the case against you. A record will be made of anything you say and it may be given in evidence if you are brought to trial." How the new warning erodes the presumption of innocence is not clear. The new warning, although longer, appears to be more explanatory in actual effect, and any negative applications would surely be addressed and placed in proper perspective by the barrister involved at trial. If an individual at the time of the warning could not accurately give his whereabouts at the date or time in question, what would be in jeopardy if the suspect said so? A possible scenario may be the following: "I do not remember precisely where I was on such and such a date but I will check my diary, (appointment book, etc.) and give the police a more accurate

---

[16] "Life with the Criminal Justice Act," *Independent,* 14 January 1994.

account later." Could this be used against the accused? If the trial were by judge only, it would appear that the judge would accurately assess what transpired, and if a jury were hearing the case, the accused's barrister would properly argue that his client did not make a statement at the time the "caution" was given, in order to be more accurate in his answer after checking the facts. This does not seem, in any realistic fashion, to be to the detriment of the accused. The fact, however, does remain that the accused does not have to say anything and if he desires to remain silent, the court or jury still has the right to draw any inference it wishes from such silence. Is that not what is done when the situation is viewed realistically? Besides, at the time the warning is given, if the accused does not understand something, he is not precluded from asking for clarification. If the individual is guilty, he incurs no harm, and if innocent, this warning could help him from appearing guilty.

Charles Glass of the *Independent* waxes quite indignant in his article headlined "A Modern Enactment of the Star Chamber.[17] It is Glass' position that the new warning overturns the right to remain silent. The research does not agree that this is the case. Nowhere is the accused forced to speak. The new warning only includes that which was a part of the legal liabilities one already faced within the system. Mr. Glass' comparison to the Star Chamber, where torture was a normal part of the legal exercise, of the new wording borders on hysteria. Glass' statement "This threat is as coercive, though not as brutal, as torture. The police and the court are saying: 'If you do not speak, you will most likely be convicted for it.'"[18] The paraphrase that Glass makes is wrong, and he adopts the language "most likely" making his a position in the extreme! Glass furthers his point that juries must consider that the testimony of the accused is now given under threat of imprisonment and is, therefore, less reliable than testimony freely given. His position is more philosophical than realistic given the fact that, in court, evidence is challenged by both sides to determine its accuracy or reliability. Moreover, Glass ignores the fact that if a confession or statement is truly coerced, it will be deemed so in the *voire dire* process prior to trial. Furthermore, from where does Glass obtain the "threat of imprisonment" which was so compelling that it produces, spontaneously, a confession?

---

[17] "A Modern Enactment of the Star Chamber," *Independent*, 9 November 1994.
[18] Ibid.

The hysteria over the issue of modifying the manner in which the "caution" was worded is perhaps best illustrated by the article appearing in the May 14, 1994 issue of the *Economist*. This issue raises several points that need careful examination. The first of these is the point of view held by some Tories, as well as Labour and Liberal Democrats in the House of Lords, that the new "caution" will require the suspect to now prove his own innocence. This clearly is not the case. The "warning" is given prior to trial and at that point in the investigation where the subject becomes a viable suspect. If the "warning" was in the original format, is it inconceivable that some, many, or even all the jurors would draw some inference from the failure of the defendant to take the stand in his own defense? Another point of contention in this article is the claim that the outcome of the new "caution" will not help in the fight against crime. How can the press be so omniscient as to determine what will occur when the new "caution" becomes law? There is clearly no data to support their theory (opinion!). Another strawman argument in the same article attempts to show that, when the right to silence was weakened in Northern Ireland as an aid to combatting terrorism, the following statistics emerged. Prior to the change of the wording of the "caution," in Northern Ireland 6.5 percent of the 3000 people prosecuted for serious or terrorist offenses were acquitted. In the five years following the change, 9 percent were acquitted. The article contends that there was no evidence that eroding the right to silence made convictions easier. The article failed to note that perhaps the new "caution" was *more* beneficial to the accused, resulting in *fewer* convictions! Though this seems implausible, the article went even further. Studies by psychologists were included to bear out the point that, under pressure of a fierce interrogation, almost everyone, however intelligent and lucid, could be made to say things they do not know to be true. The operative word here is "fierce." This conveniently overlooks the fact that the accused can still refuse to speak. How the jump from a "change in wording" to a "fierce interrogation" is made is unclear. Additionally, there is concern expressed that, without the right to silence, there is *greater* risk that the police will force wrong information from a suspect. On the face of this statement all appears correct. However, how does one admit to knowledge of a crime in which one was not involved? It is one thing to admit having committed crime such and such. However, when one commits a crime one has intimate knowledge of the details. Let us envision this scenario. A murder is committed in the victim's home. A person, not involved, would be hard pressed to provide various details. In which room did the murder take place? What was the weapon used? What were the injuries inflicted? How many? How was the victim dressed? Manner of entry into the home, etc.? Arguments by the less informed into the nature of criminal investigation do not have the knowledge to properly envision that which takes place in these circumstances of committing a crime, and then supporting the confession to the crime by being able to provide information of which only the perpetrator could have knowledge. Can the wrong person possibly confess to a crime he did not commit and be convicted for it? Yes, the possibility will always exist, but to suggest that someone would confess after coercion in a police interview room and then repeat that confession at *voire dire* prior to trial forces one to believe more in the unusual rather than the actual. Then, the article declares that the right to silence is being abolished. This is not the case. Can abuses by police contaminate an investigation? Clearly the answer is "yes," but that is an entirely different problem for, if the corruption of the police were that widespread, the matter of a mere "caution" would pale in its insignificance. This is not to minimize possible police misconduct, but rather to ensure that any misconduct is kept in its proper perspective, that it is indeed rare for such misconduct to be carried out and, if such misconduct were widespread, the population would have serious political concerns, requiring an immediate change of political direction.

Articles such as these assist in the assessment of the political climate of the population and to witness any changes brought about through political/legislative activity. The problem arises if the media indicates population directions that are not consistent with the dynamic direction as reported.

Areas of Concern

Balance in the ramification of self-incrimination is difficult to achieve. If we examine the Serious Fraud Office's powers in investigating financial criminal activity, we find a curious dilemma. Those suspects interviewed (interrogated) by the Serious Fraud Office investigators must answer questions put to them under pain of contempt. Information obtained under these conditions can be used against the suspect in subsequent criminal proceedings. This appears to be violating the basic principle of the right to silence. Carrying the thought one step further, it is easy to see that someone who kills many people has better "rights" of protection than someone possibly guilty of fraud.

Law correspondent Bruce McKain's[19] article points out that the new "caution" may face legal/political problems because the new "caution" may be in conflict with the European Convention on Human Rights. The government's position rests upon the desire to balance the rights of the individual and the need to convict the guilty. If this is the case, several questions emerge. First, is this a solution for a non-existent problem? There is no apparent entity, for neither the criminal justice system nor the population are complaining. Second, are there any data illustrating how many guilty parties were acquitted by their exercise of the "right to silence?" Finally, who and how would we define what the correct balance should be?

Perhaps it is the presumption of innocence that is the problem. This presumption places the State in the questionable position of putting on trial persons who are presumed to be innocent. What real difference would be made by a presumption of guilt? The State would still have to prove its case.

If we consider the viewpoint of the European Convention, sovereignty issues come to the fore. The new European Convention blankets the signatories with a legal concept that is homogeneous in nature. Any apparent conflict between one country's laws and the European Convention guidelines will witness those guidelines to prevail over the country's laws. The political struggle between trade conventions with the mainland would begin to conflict with the desire to deal effectively with the criminal element in England.

If the role of the European Convention was to usurp areas of sovereignty, one would find that the wording is very careful in matters to which it will or will not address itself. Article 177 (2) of the EEC Treaty states the following as outlined in *The Modern English Legal System.* "It seems that any institution which exercises judicial or quasi-judicial functions and which has at least 'a measure of official recognition' will be included, and not therefore, bodies whose functions are advisory, investigatory, conciliatory, legislative or executive."[20]

---

[19] "Scots Law Experts Question Need For Silence Rule Change." *Glasgow Herald*, 28 October 1994. sec. B, p.1.

[20] P.E. Smith and S.H. Bailey, *The Modern English Legal System* (London: Sweet & Maxwell, 1984), p. 751.

One possible solution to the use of the new wording might be to have a solicitor present at the time the "caution" is presented. This would allow for the suspect to make a better informed decision regarding his peril if he remains silent, by the possible adverse inference that could be drawn.

Who is more frightened or placed at risk by the new caution? Is it the individual whose protection is the concern of the media? Or is it the legion of lawyers fearing a loophole to the appeals court is being closed? It may, perhaps, be the political agenda of that portion of the media which is most liberal in its political viewpoint. If the new "caution" provides further legal insight to the accused, more protection is afforded him. Keeping silent on matters of possible outcomes detrimental to the accused extends little real protection. If the consequences of his silence are explained to him as possibly being negative in their effect on him, is this any different from the police advising someone not to commit any crime because of its negative consequences as well? If the police can "caution" someone as to their "right to remain silent" should they not also be permitted to issue further warnings especially if the suspect, in exercising his right, could be placing himself in jeopardy? With the new "caution", it appears the suspect is just a better informed individual.

These circumstances appear to be a result of the courts being more involved in the actual process of stationhouse actions rather than being focused on whether the confession of the accused was voluntary. The courts went out of their way to ensure that any confession forthcoming was a result of the accused harboring pangs of guilt or remorse vis-a-vis as a result of any promise or threat. This sets up a curious situation. What types of threats are inadmissible? What admissible? It would appear that a statement (threat?) by the police, that the accused would be tried for the crime, could be construed as a threat. But, is that not the reason for the investigation of a crime? To bring wrongdoers to justice? Clearly, threats of physical harm by the authorities should be excluded, as well as their actual infliction, but are there not "permissible" statements that could be labeled as "threats" merely because they produce fear of future consequences? What about "promises."? Why is it not permissible for the police to advise the suspect that his cooperation, in the form of a confession, may result in a lesser sentence if this may be the case? Is this not in the best interest of the suspect? There is argument to the effect that this scenario would defeat the voluntariness rule of admitting the confession. How so? The suspect received his "caution" and various outcomes were discussed. Again, is the suspect not now better informed? If the suspect committed the crime he is no *more* guilty than before the "caution" and attendant dialogue took place. If the forthcoming confession is questioned as to its reliability because of any promise or threat, what would be the harm to explore the totality of the circumstances at *voire dire*? Advocation for reverting to Star Chamber procedures is not the intent here but, rather, a rational look at where the English law is at present from where it originated concerning such matters.

Some recent polling data is worth including here. The results of a public opinion poll conducted by the *Independent*[21] indicates a definite shift in opinion. The "deliberative poll," described earlier in the research, bore the following fruit.

Prior to the discussion periods, the participants were asked certain questions:

A.　Should a confession made during police questioning be enough on its own to provide a conviction:

Prior to discussion	67 percent answered yes
After discussion	78 percent answered yes

B.　If the suspect remained silent under police questioning, should this be held against the suspect:

Prior to discussion	36 percent answered yes
After discussion	49 percent answered yes

On this question of the suspect remaining silent at trial, counting against the suspect:

Prior to discussion	57 percent
After discussion	41 percent

C.　Is it a worse thing to convict the innocent than to let the guilty go free:

Prior to discussion	60 percent answered yes
After discussion	70 percent answered yes

This last question had the possibility of being influenced by the manner in which the panel of experts addressed the discussion group, demonstrating in part how the police could put someone under pressure during questioning.

Another indication from the survey showed that, although the prior figures would indicate a "liberal" outlook, the respondents still held the view that the court

---

[21] "Crime/what the country really thinks; Suspects Rights/ Support for option to remain silent grows." *Independent*, 9 May, 1994, Deliberative Polling page.

process is slanted towards the accused. An increase of 11 percentage points between the surveys in the number of people who believed the courts should be less "on the side" of the accused may be reflecting a desire for a more effective system in dealing with crime.

Paul Cassell's *Miranda's Social Cost*[22] was consulted on various levels. This definitive work successfully repudiated the opinions of various writers who, during the last quarter of a century, saw little harm to the efforts of law enforcement caused by the Miranda rule. The drop in confession rate for many of the United States cities was compared in his work. Other comparisons in this work consider cases "lost" because of Miranda, with the comparisons being made across time, jurisdictions and offenses. The final analysis of his research will be discussed further in the final chapter. Additionally, Mr. Cassell and Bret Hayman[23] reviewed police questioning in another study. In this study, confession rates were compared to those of other countries, and of particular interest were those comparisons made with England and Canada showing the effects in those countries that "cautions" or "Miranda warnings" had on confession rates.

Of added value to the present research is Cassell's research in the comparisons made between the United States and England/Scotland. These confession rates are substantially higher than the United States rates post-Miranda. However, the British type Miranda in place for this table excludes the right to counsel warning that Miranda conveys. In 1984, the English employed a change in the warning which included the right to counsel as well as the recording of interrogations. The study which Cassell relies upon for his research indicating a drop in confession rates after 1984 was authored by Gisl Gudjonsson.[24] That research showed "the frequency with which suspects confess to crimes in England has fallen in recent years from over 60 percent to between 40 and 50 percent.[25] This tracks very well with the post-Miranda research conducted by Cassell. The controlling effect appears to be the inclusion of a right to counsel.

---

[22] Paul G. Cassell, "Miranda's Social Cost: An Empirical Reassessment," *Northwestern University Law Review* Vol. 90, No. 2: (1996) 391-499.

[23] Paul G. Cassell and Bret S. Hayman, "Police Interrogation in the 1990's: An Empirical Study of the Effects of Miranda," *43 UCLA Law Review* 001 (1996): 1-103.

[24] Ibid. p. 421. Cited by Cassell as Gisl H. Gudjonsson, *The Psychology of Interrogations, Confessions and Testimony* 324 (1992).

[25] Ibid. p. 421.

TABLE 5

CONFESSION RATES IN BRITAIN PRIOR TO
PACE 1984

BRITAIN - Prior to PACE 1984	Incriminating Statements Obtained
Cases Old Bailey	76%
Worcester	86%
Brighton	65%
West Yorkshire	61%
Nottinghamshire	61%
Avon	61%
Somerset	61%
Metro Police (London)	61%
(Seven Crown Court Centers) (London)	71.2%
Random selection Sheffield	94%

It is readily apparent that the variety of legal appellate points found in the United States does not enjoy similar popularity in England. The two systems also view the rights of the accused to remain silent slightly differently, the difference being that in England there is a detrimental effect upon the accused's insistence on silence. The silence of the accused can be the sole corroborating evidence needed to convict the accused. Likewise, the jury can make adverse inference from the accused's implementation of his right not to speak. This is balanced by the accused being able to use England's version of *voire dire* with some measure of protection. The appellate process in England, however, also supported the law's provision that failure to submit "exemplars" was equally considered as corroborative evidence needed to secure conviction.

The news media portrayed the "new caution" as the precursor to the collapse of the entire English judicial system, thereby allowing the media to extend its support for the accused and its opposition to the Conservative Government. The deliberative poll conducted by the media supported the fact that the impression of the people was that the court system leaned too heavily in its protection of the accused.

The most noted variance between the United States and English systems is the fundamental difference of judicial pathways. England is more straightforward by virtue of its unitary system over the entire country. In the United States, conflict has arisen over issues of legal prominence of state law versus Federal law. This process is further confused by the United States Supreme Court overriding some of its previous decisions on comparable issues.

CHAPTER 6
THE SUPREME COURT'S RULING AND THE BILL OF RIGHTS

Exactly what was it that prompted this protection of the right to remain silent? With John Lilburn, we have the scenario of a man before the awesome power of the Star Chamber defying the tribunal. He just refused to say anymore than he did, challenging his captors to charge him with evidence that they had obtained independently of his testimony, as he would offer nothing new with which they might condemn him. The earlier extremes of obtaining a confession must surely have frightened, to some degree, all those who were aware of the power of torture and their own limited willingness to experience it.

The final analysis of the research attempts to draw together those foundations that underpin the rights offered. What are the trade-offs bound within each of the two systems in question? Of relative concern is also the type of interpretation of the right to silence and those risks, if any, inherent to its use. Is the protection granted under each system the same, or does one system allow for more encroachment than the other upon the right in question? If the rights are so protected, do they benefit scoundrels or innocent people? In this area, are the dangers real or perceived when they are voiced in opposition to any revision in the wording?

Modern science has created methods of truth-finding well beyond the imagination of early protectors of the individual. What if truth could be detected without pain? How would this alter the right to silence? There are several problems with Wigmore's contention as to what is testimony, and some additional viewpoints need to be offered. There are, as well, other portions of the Fifth Amendment that are not absolute. Does this portend changes in the manner in which future right to silence arguments are decided by the Supreme Court?

With the "Miranda warning," and the "caution" in England taken as a whole, is there a better protection which should be considered as being more effective to the suspect? In this chapter, research which examines the societal cost of "warnings" as well as the impact under each system upon law enforcement, will be reviewed.

Outside the spectacle of legal wrangling is the matter of society itself, that body politic which wagers in the lottery of government by its selection of representatives to become the gatherers of trust in order to provide for the safety of the citizens while balancing the rights of other citizens suspected of crime.

A clearer picture of what exactly "rights" are, and how they are viewed is, perhaps, to examine them in comparison to other rights and how they have been interpreted. This is required because not all rights are treated (interpreted) in the same manner, and some rights have been handled more than others by the Supreme Court over the years. If these rights have been expanded or contracted by the various interpretations, has this strengthened the provisions of each right?

We will start with the First Amendment. The concept of freedom of the press, speech, religion and assembly are purely the child of American political thought. Whereas other provisions in the Bill of Rights have deep roots in English law and tradition, the close relationship in England between politics and the Church provided fertile ground for censorship and political repression of opposition. The history of the period of 1585, with its Star Chamber in ascendence, clearly shows how printed material could not be published until it was reviewed and licensed by the Archbishop or his delegate. Although these licensing laws were abolished in 1594, this did not lead to a burgeoning society openly expressing free thought. There were still in effect very stringent libel and sedition codes which were rigorously enforced.

After the United States Constitution was ratified, additional measures were needed to protect the *individual* from governmental oppression. In order to ensure that the individual could be secure in his dealings with the Government, certain "protections" were expressed in a Bill of Rights. The importance of free speech, press, religion and assembly were considered the most important, for without these firmly enshrined, other provisions would be meaningless. An area free from Federal control, that of intellectual freedom, was created.

The population of the United States is a heterogeneous one. As a natural consequence of its diverse groupings one finds the various needs of each group, each competing for limited resources and each, in turn, criticizing the Government for its failure to provide to that group that which the group considers its just due.

"Congress shall make no law . . . abridging the freedom of speech." If one now considers Wigmore's position of testimony being speech only, and with the United

States Supreme Court essentially concurring with that notion, one should now view the Supreme Court and its views on speech vis-a-vis the First Amendment. If one is to examine this provision, "speech" must first be involved. If one burns a draft card, is that "speech?" If it is burned in silence, is that speech? Is nude dancing "speech?" Further, does the challenge to the *act* constitute an abridgement of free speech? If the restriction of these acts is based in aspects of communication (messages, political expression, etc.) then possible conflict with the First Amendment could occur. Can the Government force people to speak? Can the Government force citizens to dance, burn draft cards or voice those beliefs which the population finds abhorrent?[1] If these instances are protected by free speech and the First Amendment, there is small room for acceptance in the Fifth Amendment to not consider the drawing of blood as being a witness against oneself i.e. giving testimony -- speech! Nor can it provide for silence for prayer or meditation. The First Amendment includes ideologically grounded silence as well.[2] If the various nuances of so-called speech can be considered, such as boycotts, pickets, parades, letter-writing, media broadcasting and live entertainment, how then can Wigmore and his interpretations of the Fifth Amendment hold up? Are not all the provisions of the Bill of Rights of equal weight in their application to the individual vis-a-vis the Government? In the case of the First Amendment, language is not an indispensable ingredient to afford constitutional protection.

The Second Amendment states, in part ". . . the right of the people to have and bear arms, shall not be infringed." It is curious to note that, in dealing with the Second Amendment, we find that the Supreme Court, in *Presser v. Illinois*[3] issued a rather peculiar ruling. The Court held that the Second Amendment only restricts the Federal Government, and therefore a state or city ordinance does not necessarily conflict with the Constitution in regulating who may or may not possess handguns.

The research find this curious in that the Federal courts have asserted their authority to enforce laws through the vehicle of the Fourteenth Amendment, extending Federal safeguards to the individual when state laws would be more

---

[1] West Virginia State Board of Education v. Burnette 319 U.S. 624, 63 S. Ct. 1178, 87 L. Ed. 1628 (1943). In this case, the Supreme Court struck down a state statute requiring school children to pledge their allegiance to and salute the flag.

[2] Wallace v. Jeffries, 472 U.S. 38, 105 S. Ct. 2749, 86 L. Ed. 2nd 29 (1985).

[3] Presser v. Illinois, 116 U.S. 252, 6 S. Ct. 580, 29 L. Ed. 615 (1886).

restrictive or oppressive. Presser clearly shows that the Supreme Court does not unilaterally extend solid Constitutional guarantees equally, but rather, the protections granted are on a case-by-case (direction of political wind?) basis. If this is so, other provisions are in no less of a precarious situation.

The Third Amendment addresses the issue of quartering troops in one's home during peace or war. This has not yet been considered a problem of note.

Prior to the Revolutionary War, England issued to various individuals Writs of Assistance. These were, for the most part, general search warrants allowing the holder to search for smuggled goods. Broad powers were granted with these Writs, and they became the outrage of the citizenry because of their issuance. The Fourth Amendment was to be a safeguard against unreasonable searches and seizures. The case law surrounding this Amendment soon erodes the Court's position allowing the states a free hand in matters of searches and seizures. The final peg is the attachment of the Fourteenth Amendment to the Fourth Amendment guaranteeing that the states' excesses would not erode the provisions granted by the Fourth Amendment. The Writs of Assistance, which covered arrests on mere suspicion, was another provision the Fourth Amendment sought to guard against. The case/argument against the Writs of Assistance pre-dated by four years the Stamp Act which was, perhaps, more important in helping to shape constitutional issues. But, "John Adams, eager to secure pride of place in the Revolution for Massachusetts was obsessed with the case."[4] Adams wrote, sixty years later, "Then and there was the scene of the first Act of Opposition to the arbitrary claims of Great Britain."[5] This was the first articulation of the American viewpoint, which still lingers, demonstrating opposition to general warrants used for search. Although the Constitution did not allow for unlawful searches/seizures up until 1914, all evidence was essentially admitted into court. In *Weeks v. United States*, 1914,[6] the Supreme Court held that letters belonging to the defendant were illegally seized by Federal officers and the Supreme Court ruled that, in a Federal prosecution, the Fourth Amendment barred the use of illegally obtained

---

[4] Hendrik Hartog, ed., *Law in the American Revolution and the Revolution in the Law: A Collection of Review Essays on American Legal History*, New York University School of Law Series in Legal History, no. 3 (New York: New York University Press, 1981), p. 4.
[5] Ibid.
[6] Weeks v. United States, 232 U.S. 383, 34 S. Ct. 341, 58 L. Ed. 652 (1914).

evidence. This however, left open the door for state officers to continue not observing the Fourth amendment if it so pleased them.

As mentioned earlier in the research, this attitude allowed the "silver platter" doctrine to come into play, where state officers could obtain evidence in the fashion they did, the Fourth Amendment notwithstanding. Once obtained by the state officers, the evidence could be passed to Federal officers without Fourth Amendment violation. This situation prevailed until the Supreme Court ruled in *Elkins v. United States*.[7] After Elkins, the Federal courts could not use any illegally seized evidence, regardless of the source providing it to the Federal prosecutors or courts.

What is curious is the ruling in *Wolf v. Colorado* (1949)[8] which, at that time, ruled that the "exclusionary rule" would apply to the states' courts. A vote on the "exclusionary rule" across the country showed thirty-one state courts did not like the rule and sixteen states were in favor of adopting it into their state laws. A summarizing thought from Wolf is illustrative. "We hold, therefore, that in a prosecution in a State court for a State crime the Fourteenth Amendment does not forbid the admission of evidence obtained by unreasonable search and seizure."[9]

Closure appeared to be at hand with the *Mapp v. Ohio*[10] case. In this case, the Supreme Court overruled its earlier decision in Wolf and declared that the provisions of the Fourth Amendment did apply to the states by reason of the Fourteenth Amendment. There were only twelve years between Wolf and Mapp, and yet, what was so clear in Wolf still gave way to the decision in Mapp. Clearly, the Supreme Court was edging toward a more intrusive role in states' affairs. What is more noteworthy, perhaps, is the ease with which the Supreme Court "gives" and "takes away" its favors. In this case, the accused is better protected, but the thought must be considered that a more conservative, or law and order disposed, majority of the Court has within its grasp the wherewithal to view the protection in a more restrictive manner.

The Fifth Amendment is well presented throughout the research and is not included here at this time for comparison purposes.

---

[7] Elkins v. United States, 364 U.S. 206, 80 S. Ct. 1437, 4 L. Ed. 2d 1669 (1960).
[8] Wolf v. Colorado, 338 U.S. 25, 69 S. Ct. 1359, 93 L. Ed. 1782 (1949).
[9] Ibid.
[10] Mapp v. Ohio, 367 U.S. 643, 81 S. Ct. 1684, 6 L. Ed. 2d 1081, (1961).

An additional provision of the Fifth Amendment not yet considered in the research concerns "double jeopardy," that provision which prohibits re-trials for the same offence. It provides "that no person shall be subject for the same offence to be twice put in jeopardy of life or limb." This protection dates back in English law to the thirteenth century, so it was common practice long before colonial laws were enacted in the United States. Bartkus' decision[11] by the Supreme Court underlined the accepted practice, however, of allowing *two* different jurisdictions (state and Federal) to each try a defendant for the same crime if each judicial system listed the act as proscribed by law. If an accused can be tried by both systems, it is difficult to understand what interests of the accused this restraint is designed to protect. The obvious ones include protecting the defendant from continued financial costs in subsequent trials if the accused could be tried, after being acquitted in the same court system, by that same system. The emotional protection is a given for the same set of circumstances. Any protection, however, does not come to the fore until the accused has reached that point in the judicial proceedings where he is actually placed in jeopardy. That point is reached in jury trials when the jury is empaneled and sworn, and in bench trials when testimony has begun to be heard -- jeopardy being here defined as the risk of conviction and punishment.[12] The provisions state jeopardy of life or limb, but in reality, this protection is extended to all criminal trials, both misdemeanor and felony. The protection is not extended to civil proceedings even when the Government is the plaintiff.[13]

There are other circumstances where an accused can be re-tried. They are:

A.   Where the accused requests and is granted a termination of his first trial before the charges against him are resolved

B.   where the trial judge prematurely halts the first trial for reasons of "manifest necessity"

C.   where the accused's conviction is set aside by appeal

One fact does remain however. If the accused is acquitted, it does not matter that the acquittal was a result of mistaken rulings, misinterpretation of criminal statutes or on

---

[11] Bartkus v. Illinois, 359 U.S. 121, 79 S. Ct. 676, 2 L. Ed. 2d 684 (1959). (Black, J. dissenting).

[12] Breed v. Jones, 421 U.S. 519, 95 S. Ct. 1779, 44 L. Ed. 2d 346 (1975).

[13] One Lot Emerald Cut Stones and One Ring v. United States, 409 U.S. 232, 93 S. Ct. 489, 34 L. Ed. 2d 438 (1972).

trial errors, retrial for the same offence following acquittal is constitutionally prohibited.[14] A curious point surfaces with regard to "double jeopardy" and dual sovereignty. If an accused can be prosecuted for the same crime under different judicial systems because the offense was proscribed by each, how then can the Supreme Court turn its back on those states which, in state law violations, elect not to follow Miranda guidelines? If the Constitution reaches out through the Fourteenth Amendment in matters of search and seizure (remembering the Silver Platter doctrine), how can the Court then reconcile double jeopardy as being outside the Federal/state guidelines vis-a-vis the Bill of Rights and the Fourteenth Amendment? The case can be made that the Supreme Court either treats each Amendment differently, or, the Court differing over time views the protections granted by the Bill of Rights with greater or lesser importance.

The Sixth Amendment can be reduced to its pertinent provision "In all criminal prosecutions, the accused shall enjoy the right . . . to have the assistance of Counsel for his defense." This provision or protection has been expanded as well. It is well to note that the denial of counsel at the time of interrogation nullifies the confession, thus underscoring the protection offered. There are various Court decisions extending the right to counsel, starting with "the preliminary hearing . . . if counsel is not afforded to the accused at this 'critical stage' of the proceedings a plea of guilty at a later future trial will be disallowed." The same reasoning applies to the arraignment and, of course, to the actual trial itself. This is true, even if there is no apparent unfairness in the proceedings.[15] The question, prior to 1938, was concerned with whether the provision imposed an affirmative obligation on the part of the court to appoint counsel, where the accused does not request counsel or if he is unable to pay for one. Further, did this provision address felony cases or "capital" cases only? In 1938, the Supreme Court issued its decision in *Johnson v. Zerbst.*[16] In all Federal trials of persons charged with crimes of a serious nature, counsel must be appointed for an indigent defendant unless he intelligently waives his right to counsel. An

---

[14] Fong Foo v. United States, 369 U.S. 141, 82 S. Ct. 671, 7 L. Ed. 2d 629 (1962). Also Green v. United States, 355 U.S. 184, 78 S. Ct. 221, 2 L. Ed. 2d 199 (1957). Also Kepner v. United States, 195 U.S. 100, 24 S. Ct. 797, 49 L. Ed. 114 (1904).

[15] Ferguson v. Georgia, 365 U.S. 570, 81 S. Ct. 756, 5 L. Ed. 2d 793 (1961).

[16] Johnson v. Zerbst, 304 U.S. 458, 58 S. Ct. 1019, 82 L. Ed. 1461 (1938).

earlier case of *Powell v. Alabama*[17] provided for Federal standards in state courts dealing with "capital" crimes. Some twelve years elapsed until *Betts v. Brady* (1942)[18] entertained the issue of including state felony crimes under the umbrella of the Sixth Amendment. At that time, the Supreme Court did *not* incorporate the state courts to provide counsel for non-capital felony cases. Indeed, it was not until 1963, under the same Supreme Court that expanded the rights of a suspect, and which would go on in 1964 to write the decisions in Escobedo and Miranda, that the state courts were tied to the Sixth Amendment through the auspices of the Fourteenth Amendment in *Gideon v. Wainwright* (1963).[19] This case overruled Betts and its prior Supreme Court decision, and now the Court provided to the accused that which an earlier Court denied him. The right to counsel was now firmly fixed for trial purposes. Could the accused now petition for representation by counsel at other preliminary stages of the process? The Sixth Amendment itself gives little guidance, granting only that the accused should enjoy the right to counsel in all "criminal prosecutions." Is the prosecution of an accused the trial itself or is it all-encompassing from start to finish? The research now looks to *Hamilton v. Alabama.*[20] This case examined the right to counsel at the arraignment of the accused. This last step prior to trial advises the accused of his right to counsel; he is informed of the charges against him and he is given an opportunity to enter a plea. The Supreme Court held in Hamilton that the arraignment was so critical a stage that, if the accused were to be denied counsel at this juncture, it would be tantamount to denial of due process of law. In a period of less than twenty years, the right to counsel was extended to cover right to counsel in all felony trials, then to the arraignment stage and ultimately, to the preliminary hearing. Progression continued backwards in the criminal justice process to go on to include the investigatory phase with Escobedo.[21] In this case, Escobedo was arrested and released on habeas corpus the same day. Arrested again eleven days later, Escobedo requested an opportunity to consult with his lawyer, who was also attempting to contact his client. The police were able to frustrate their meeting together, and incriminating statements were made

---

[17] Powell v. Alabama, 287 U.S. 45, 53 S. Ct. 55, 77 L. Ed. 2d 158 (1932).
[18] Betts v. Brady, 316 U.S. 455, 465, 62 S. Ct. 1252, 86 L. Ed. 1595 (1942).
[19] Gideon v. Wainwright, 372, U.S. 335, 83 S. Ct. 792, 9 L. Ed. 2d 799 (1963).
[20] Hamilton v. Alabama, 368 U.S. 52, 82 S. Ct. 157, 7 L. Ed. 2d 114 (1961).
[21] Escobedo v. Illinois, 378 U.S. 478, 84 S. Ct. 1758, 12 L. Ed. 2d 977 (1964).

by Escobedo. Escobedo went to trial and was convicted. His conviction was overturned five to four by the United States Supreme Court. Justice Goldberg wrote the majority decision, stating "When the process shifts from the investigatory to the accusatory . . . the accused must be permitted to consult with his lawyer." The Miranda case cited earlier in the research was the next logical step. This progression put the Sixth Amendment and the Fifth amendment in lock-step with each other. There are some state cases wherein the accused was not allowed counsel for a psychiatric examination. The ruling of the United States Court of Appeals Fifth Circuit stated that " a psychiatric examination is not an adversary proceeding."[22] Right to counsel now extends to the line-up procedure (*United States v. Wade*),[23] or in-court identification (*Gilbert v. California*).[24] And, identification procedures prior to charging the accused (*Kirby v. Illinois*)[25] are not covered by the Sixth Amendment. These cases presented were all of a felony nature. It was the case of *Argersinger v. Hamlin*[26] that saw the United States Supreme Court attack the Sixth Amendment in misdemeanor cases where a possible outcome, if the accused is convicted, is imprisonment. On May 15, 1967, the Supreme Court of the United States extended the right-to-counsel privilege to juveniles.[27] Also now included were:

A.   Right to counsel on appeal[28]

B.   Right to counsel at probation or parole revocation hearing[29]

C.   Effective assistance of counsel[30]

D.   Right to freely communicate with counsel[31]

E.   Self-representation rights[32]

---

[22] United States v. Williams, 456 F. 2d 217 (5th Cir. 1972). Also: Stultz v. State, 500 S.W. 2d 853 (Tex. 1973).

[23] United States v. Wade, 388 U.S. 218, 87 S. Ct. 1926, 18 L. Ed. 2d 1149 (1967).

[24] Gilbert V. California, 388 U.S. 263, 87 S. Ct. 1951, 18 L. Ed. 2d 1178 (1967).

[25] Kirby v. Illinois, 406 U.S. 682, 92 S. Ct. 1877, 32 L. Ed. 2d 411 (1972).

[26] Argersinger v. Hamlin, 407 U.S. 25, 92 S. Ct. 2006, 32 L. Ed. 2d 530 (1972).

[27] In Re Gault, 387 U.S.L, 87 S. Ct. 1428, 18 L. Ed. 2d 527 (1967).

[28] Douglas v. California, 372 U.S. 353, 83 S. Ct. 814, 9 L. Ed. 2d 811 (1963).

[29] Mempa v. Rhay, 389 U.S. 128, 88 S. Ct. 254, 19 L. Ed. 2d 336 (1967).

[30] Cardarell v. United States, 375 F. 2d 222 (8th Cir. 1967) quoting O'Malley v. United States, 285 F. 2d 733, 734 (6th Cir. 1961).

[31] State *Ex Rel.* Tucker v. Davis, 9 Okla. Crim. 94, 130 P. 962 (1913). Also State v. Cory, 62 Wash. 2d 371, 382 P. 2d 1019 (1963).

[32] Faretta v. California, 422 U.S. 806, 95 S. Ct. 2525, 45 L. Ed. 2d 562 (1975).

The Sixth Amendment providing a speedy trial, and the right to trial by jury are unremarkable, with the possible exception of unanimous verdicts by the jury being a prerequisite to conviction. Two states allow for less than unanimous verdicts. They are Louisiana[33] and Oregon.[34] The Supreme Court in a five to four decision in *Apodaca v. Oregon*[35] upheld that in *state* courts unanimous verdicts were not required by the Sixth Amendment. Mr. Justice Powell, who provided the swing vote, stated that whereas in Federal proceedings unanimous verdicts were an indispensable part of the Sixth Amendment. However, he rejected as unsound the premise that, when a given procedural safeguard is incorporated into the Fourteenth Amendment and made binding upon state jurisdictions, *identical* (emphasis author) state application is required. Here again, it appears that state/Federal viewpoints are not congruent by law. However, this provision for less than unanimous verdicts did not survive in six-man juries utilizing a five out of six requirement for conviction. In *Burch v. Louisiana*,[36] the Supreme Court ruled that a non-unanimous six-person jury presented a sufficient threat to the fairness of the proceedings and the proper functioning of the jury to draw the Constitutional line. In direct contrast to holdings of the Supreme Court in regards to the Fifth Amendment, the Supreme Court, in addressing issues of the Sixth Amendment, has ruled that the Government may *not* compel a criminal defendant to stand trial before a jury while dressed in prison garments, because this practice served no important *Governmental* interest.[37] In *Holt v. United States*, discussed earlier in the research, the United States Supreme Court held that the Governmental interest should prevail (1910) and allowed the defendant to be dressed as requested by the state. Whether Estelle overturned Holt is unclear. What is being considered is the point that, if protections are expanded or restricted, are these expansions/contractions in themselves amending the Amendments? If so, then it appears that "judicial review" in the United States has taken on a legislative role and that would be contrary to the role authorized by the Constitution itself.

In consideration of the argument that is fostered by Wigmore in regards to speech and testimony questioned earlier, this question requires attention in rebuttal.

---

[33] LA. Code Crim. Proc. Ann. art. 782 (West 1966).

[34] Or. Const. art. I, Para. II; Or. Rev. stat. Paras. 136. 330, (1967).

[35] Apodaca v. Oregon, 406 U.S. 404, 92 S. Ct. 1628, 32 L. Ed. 2d 184 (1972).

[36] Burch v. Louisiana, 441 U.S. 130, 99 S. Ct. 1623, 60 L. Ed. 2d 96 (1979).

[37] Estelle v. Williams, 425 U.S. 96 S. Ct. 1691, 48 L. Ed. 2d 126 (1976).

The Eighth Amendment forbids "cruel and unusual" punishment. In *Furman v. Georgia*, Justice Brennan traced the history of the Eighth Amendment relating to punishment to include, at the time the Bill of Rights was written, public hanging, flogging, cropping of ears, etc. Thomas Jefferson himself advocated castration, facial mutilation, etc. for those convicted of rape, sodomy or polygamy. These punishments were not considered unusual or cruel at that time. Investigation of the case *Weems v. United States*[38] finds the Court resorting to phrases such as "expansive and vital character" and capacity for "evolutionary growth"[39] thereby expanding cruel punishment to be viewed in the context of contemporary standards. If punishment is to be viewed in contemporary light, and if that same contemporary light views wearing a flag of the United States on the rear portion of someone's jeans as free speech, then how can that same speech be limited to verbal testimony as according to Wigmore? If speech is "things" and "actions," then the drawing of blood (both a "thing" and an "action") must also be considered speech and protected by the Fifth Amendment. Perhaps the protection offered by the Fifth is no protection at all save to prohibit "torture" for obtaining confessions.

---

[38] Weems v. United States, 217 U.S. 349, 377, 30 S. Ct. 544, 553, 54 L. Ed. 793, 802 (1910).
[39] Trop v. Dulles, 356 U.S. 86, 78 S. Ct. 590, 2 L. Ed. 2d 630 (1958).

CHAPTER 7
PUBLIC ATTITUDES CONCERNING THE RIGHT TO SILENCE

Polls and surveys provide necessary feedback to both the government and the people. They allow for each in turn to view a given event. From the government's perspective they show how the population supports or rejects proposed revisions. For the public, polls and surveys give needed input to the individual that he might make comparison of his opinions in relationship to the population as a whole.

The consensus of the governed, coupled with a perceived benevolent bureaucracy, help to provide the needed components for the formation of the political culture. The intertwining of values and the interaction of the competing groups can dispel anxiety and create or maintain the stability required for the population to flourish. The government, as well as the people, needs feedback on the effects of various changes in policy or law that affect the people. To accomplish this, some government agencies utilize the perspective and experiences of other countries to support their particular line of reasoning for instituting change. This, however, is only one part of the requisite equation. The missing element is perceptual knowledge of how the people are considering these changes. Miranda was to have a significant effect upon the criminal justice system of the United States. This, in turn, would impact upon the people and their perception of safety from both the government and crime. The media can play an important role in providing to the government what the people are thinking and, additionally, to the people, allowing them to assess their perspectives in relation to the remainder of the population. The media does this through polls and surveys. We will view Miranda with this in mind.

Whereas Chief Justice Warren's argument in his Miranda decision that "the experience in some other countries also suggests that the danger to law enforcement in curbs on interrogation is overplayed . . . there appears to have been no marked detrimental effect on criminal law enforcement in these jurisdictions as a result of these rules."[1]

What is clear is that Miranda obviously did affect the percentage of confessions obtained in the United States and, when England adopted similar provisions, such as the addition of a right to counsel, similarities in the rate of loss of confessions obtained were observed.

England has witnessed an erosion of the "cautioned" post 1984. The recent changes listed earlier in the research are clearly designed to balance the rights of the accused while maintaining, as a goal, the determination of facts. Only through the determination of facts can the guilty be identified, the punishment be assessed according to law and the well being of society be secured.

For purposes of this research, it must be noted that Miranda is only a Supreme Court prescription for obtaining a confession, and that the underlying protection is still the Fifth Amendment and its prohibition on coerced confessions. This is evidenced by the Court's ruling in Tucker,[2] Quarles[3] and Elstad.[4] In Tucker, the Court held, through Chief Justice Rehnquist, that the Miranda warnings were "not themselves rights protected by the Constitution" but only "prophylactic standards" designed to "safeguard" or to "provide practical reinforcement" for the privilege against self-incrimination. In Quarles, the Court also refused Quarles' contention that statements made by Quarles could be used absent Miranda warnings, taking into consideration the point that the "public safety" was paramount as well as the fact that the police did not compel him to speak nor coerce him -- only that the police failed to provide the Miranda warning. In Elstad, we have a similar circumstance in that two confessions were given, the first without Miranda and a second confession a short while later, with the Miranda warning preceding the questioning. Elstad contended that the first un-Mirandized confession contaminated the second Mirandized confession, thereby making the second confession "fruit of the poisoned tree" and therefore inadmissible. The Court disagreed saying, in essence, that the "fruit of the poisoned tree" assumes the existence of an underlying constitutional

---

[1] Paul G. Cassell. "Miranda's Social Cost: An Empirical Reassessment," *Northwestern University Law Review* Vol. 90, No. 2 (1996):418.

[2] Michigan v. Tucker, 417 U.S. 433, 94 S. Ct. 2357, 41 L. Ed. 2d 182 (1974).

[3] New York v. Quarles, 467 U.S. 649, 104 S. Ct. 2626, 81 L. Ed. 2d 550 (1984).

[4] Oregon v. Elstad, 470 U.S. 298, 105 S. Ct. 1285, 84 L. Ed. 2d 222 (1985).

violation, and that the failure to give a Miranda warning is not in itself a violation of the Fifth Amendment. "If, as the present Court seems to say, a violation of the self-incrimination clause itself occurs only when a confession is 'involuntary' under traditional standards, is this an outright rejection of the core premise of Miranda?"[5]

Perhaps the Court now sees the earlier broadness of the Miranda interpretation as flawed and is seeking pathways to politely circumvent Miranda by applying new interpretations to the rule. If the Supreme Court can revise the Amendments by the mere reinterpretation of them, then it is reasonable to assume that Miranda, being only a Court created ruling and not an Amendment, could also be re-interpreted.

The advisability of a Bill of Rights for its citizens is being examined presently by the people in England. Editorials are replete with instances where ministers have exceeded their authority. The courts are not powerless to take action as evidenced by Minister Kenneth Baker being found guilty of contempt of court for deporting an asylum seeker. An editorial in the *Independent* stated,

> By extending their powers and occasionally flouting the law, ministers have inadvertently legitimized judicial activity in areas that were once deemed the preserve of politics. If Britain gets a Bill of Rights, as Labour promises, we can expect even more aggressive intervention. . . [6]

The political position of the Tories has always been to be "tough on crime." That this is a strong political issue is evidenced by the Labour party also espousing strong measures to combat crime. So, while the newspapers and various groups oppose the new legislation of England's crime bill, both political parties appear to be of one thought as it relates to encroachment on the right of silence. The *Age* wrote, ". . . spells an end to the 300 year old right of those accused of crimes to remain silent."[7] Other comments depicting dire effects include such phrases as ". . . not only removes the right to silence and undermines presumption of innocence . . ."[8]

With Parliament being the legislative body and supreme in matters of law, the marriage of politics, legislation, social and criminal issues all come together in such

---

[5] Yale Kamisar et al., *Basic Criminal Procedure*, (St. Paul, MN: West Publishing Co., 1994), p. 505.
[6] "In Judgement of Government," *Independent*, 29 November 1994, editorial, p. 15.
[7] "Britain's New Law and Disorder," *Age*, (Melbourne), 5 November 1994, p. 26.
[8] Ibid.

a manner that it clearly shows the rapid change possible in affecting one's rights. If the social/political outcry is sufficient, then politicians, desirous of maintaining their political station and structures, must and will acquiesce to those demands voiced by their constituencies. Differing views of the public are voiced by various others such as QC Michael Mansfield who said "the bill is the most draconian act this government has put through."[9] Sir John Smith, the president of the Association of Chief Police Officers, offered that "the bill ran the risk of politicising the police and alienating communities."[10]

United States Polls and Surveys

The *Wall Street Journal* viewed public opinion on the Fifth Amendment in September, 1995. Although it would be difficult to determine how widespread the following views are, the fact remains that these views are indeed part of the public domain for discussion. The article cites the O.J. Simpson trial where, not only did the accused not testify but, a prosecution witness, Mark Furman, invoked his right to silence privilege. Edward Felsenthal, whose by-line carried this article, indicated that this use of the Fifth Amendment by Mark Furman "has done an awful lot to destroy people's confidence that the Fifth Amendment is invoked to prevent government excesses."[11] To show that this use is viewed unfavorably Felsenthal cites Washington lawyer, Harvey Pitt, who said "That's not going to be helpful in future cases where people try to invoke the Fifth Amendment."[12] This reference to prosecution witnesses has happened in the Simpson case. In the Bernard Goetz case, two of the youths shot by the so-called "subway vigilante" and who were also prosecution witnesses, took the Fifth Amendment. Boston criminal defense lawyer, Harvey Silverglate, feels that "if a plebiscite on the Fifth Amendment was held today it would likely be defeated.[13]

Here is where the Bill of Rights offers real protection. The whims of the moment of the public cannot be easily satisfied. The process necessary to change the Amendments is a long and deliberative one. To be successful, any change must have

---

[9] Ibid.
[10] Ibid.
[11] "As Fifth Amendment is Invoked More, Would Framers Rue What They Created?" *Wall Street Journal*, 12 September 1995, p. B1.
[12] Ibid.
[13] Ibid.

the support of Congress, the President and the States. There is a shorter method in form, but it is longer in the time generally spent going through the former method. This method is through interpretation by at least five members of the Supreme Court. The members of the Court are appointed for life. They leave the bench either by dying or retiring. This process has allowed, as a consequence, the ability of a president to place upon this Court his legacy, far into the future, after he himself is no longer in office. If the president, unable to place his agenda on the Court due to a lack of vacancy, tried to increase the size of the Court, he would most likely face the same fate as Franklin D. Roosevelt did in his attempt to "stack the court" in order to help with his New Deal legislation. Even the appointment of Federal judges to the various levels of the Federal judiciary has its own spheres of influence. Whereas in selecting a judge for the Supreme Court, the president selects with the advice and consent of the Senate, in the lower Federal district courts, the senators from the state in which the need exists nominate the judge with the president consenting. This "tradition" of patronage, as a perk of being a senator, came into being around 1840. The Federal Court of Appeals, which spans several states, falls again within the prerogative of the president, because different states are involved. This process of judge appointments gives diversity to the system, allowing for competing political interests to be heard. This diversity can be of great political advantage to a president. He can play one senator against another in order to increase the likelihood of his Supreme Court nominee being confirmed. A president, therefore, can nudge the political thought of the Supreme Court in his direction, if the circumstances allow enough of his input to be reflected in the make-up of the Court.

Polls and surveys are used to determine what message being put forth by the population. This manner of pulse-taking information is important to both the population and where, amongst its heirarchy of needs, it is being placed. The polls indicated here that the populations of both England and the United States viewed the "right to silence" with a similar degree of importance. Cassell's research demonstrated that, even when crime statistics were increasing, the "right to silence" suffered little in the eyes of the people. England's data showed similar concerns.

Polls can also indicate the political underpinnings of Supreme Court nominees and the ultimate outcome. In an article by E.J. Dionne, Jr., the importance of the nominee's constitutional viewpoint carries a great deal of weight.

The question of judicial philosophy has become central to the Bork nomination because Justice Powell had been a key swing vote on the Court. Liberals fear that Judge Bork would decisively move the Court to the Right. Also, many Bork opponents concede his intelligence and competence and will thus have to contest the nomination on philosophical grounds.[14]

In July, 1987, a poll taken over two days asked the following questions of seven hundred and forty-five respondents. First, was the Supreme Court too liberal or too conservative? Second, has the Supreme Court gone too far in protecting the rights of the accused? The results were that 36 percent felt the Court was too liberal; 38 percent felt the Court to be too conservative; 43 percent felt the Court went too far in protecting the rights of the accused and 41 percent felt that the Court needed to do more for the accused.

Another question in this poll addressed the issue of whether or not a nominee to the Supreme Court should be questioned on his or her judicial philosophy. Democrats answered in favor of questioning the nominee as to his/her judicial philosophy at 65 percent, Republicans at 63 percent, Liberals at 64 percent and Conservatives at 61 percent. The last question asked if the President should pay "a lot of attention" to the nominee's judicial philosophy, to which 72 percent replied that he should. No breakdown on this last question was provided as to party affiliation or political viewpoint, whether Liberal or Conservative.

"In a Times/CBS News Poll taken in June 1986, 34 percent said the Supreme Court had 'gone too far in protecting the rights of people accused of crimes.'"[15] In a 1987 repeat survey, the figure was 43 percent.

Another poll, taken in 1987, was conducted in Ohio. This Ohio poll was conducted at the University of Cincinnati's Institute for Policy Research with an accuracy rating of plus or minus 3 percent. A random selection of 818 adults were interviewed across the state between April 23rd and May 9th.[16] The questions asked were as follows:

Do you agree or disagree with the following statements?

---

[14] "Senate Should Consider the Opinions of High Court Nominees, Poll Finds." *New York Times*, 24 July 1987, sec. A, p. 12.
[15] Ibid. p. 12.
[16] "Ohioans Support Suspects' Constitutional Rights," *Regional News* (Cincinnati), 28 July, 1987. p. B4.

A.   Police should be required to warn a criminal suspect before interrogation of the right to remain silent and to have a lawyer

Agree	85 percent
Disagree	13 percent
No opinion	2 percent

B.   Evidence that proves the guilt of a suspect should be admissible in a criminal trial even if the evidence was obtained in a search that violated the individual's constitutional rights

Should be admissible	59 percent
Should not be admissible	35 percent
No opinion	6 percent

It appears the population at large fears interrogation more than intrusive searches. Could this be a reflection of the population's fear of the "third degree" methods visualized by those polled?

The American Bar Association also conducted a study addressing the exclusionary rule and the Supreme Court's Miranda decision.[17] This study, conducted over a two-year period, concluded that neither the exclusionary rule nor Miranda were hindering the police or the prosecutors from doing their job. The survey was performed by telephone and was national in scope. It contacted police, prosecutors, defense attorneys and judges. The survey concluded that the lack of adequate resources and not legal protections was the culprit in the rise of drug related cases.

On the surface, this report is easy to accept but it must be considered "soft" because rarely will an administrator state his resources are adequate for, if they are adequate, why then is he not more successful in lowering his crime rate? Budget increases are grants of power -- the bigger the budget, the more power to wield. It appears that lawyers, on either side of the issue, prefer to have cumbersome points of law to consider and argue rather than to clarify or streamline the legal system. It is also problematical for political post holders, police chiefs, prosecutors, judges, etc. to support less constitutional rights for people. It is not a good political platform to stand upon, so the safe bet is for them to take the position that resources, neutral in ideology, are the culprit.

---

[17] "Study Says Drug Crisis Overwhelming Legal System" *Associated Press*, 30 November 1988. p. A16.

The *National Law Journal* published the results, in August of 1989, of a *National Law Journal/Lexis* poll with the following results.[18] The published results failed to provide the total number of respondents to the questionnaire. The questionnaire consisted of seventy questions and covered suspects' rights, causes of crime, extent of the emergency perceived, racism, the media and Supreme Court rulings. Of interest to this research are the numbers concerned with suspects' rights and Supreme Court rulings.

Nearly half of those surveyed favored cutting back suspects' rights

34 percent felt "desperate" about crime

48 percent supported reversing court rulings that limit police conduct in gathering evidence

Another poll taken in November, 1993 indicated that, although crime was a major problem, a majority of the five hundred people surveyed would NOT support diminishing the protections currently enjoyed by suspects.

"There's a feeling that maybe something that protects an alleged criminal will protect me too," Ferrer said. "The majority is willing to let some guilty people go free rather than convict innocent people."[19]

In April of 1994, the *National Law Journal* conducted another poll to compare with the one performed in 1989. One standout feature indicated a dramatic change in numbers. Whereas in 1989, 34 percent felt "desperate" about crime and personal safety, in 1994 that figure jumped to 62 percent. "Those polled reject the government's intrusion on basic civil rights, gun ownership and the media's displays of violence."[20] It appears 78 to 85 percent of people are unwilling to give up basic civil rights even if doing so might enhance their personal safety. Another dramatic figure showed three out of four people say that the police and the criminal justice system cannot protect people adequately. Could this portend a turn to "vigilante" tactics? If so, when then does the protection for civil rights come in? The survey was perhaps too broad in its scope, thereby allowing conclusions to be drawn in

---

[18] Fred Strasser, "Perceptions and Reality; Crime in America," *National Law Journal* (7 August 1989): 52.
[19] Courant-ISI Connecticut Poll, *Hartford Courant*, 21 November 1993, A edition, p. B1.
[20] "Crime's Toll on the U.S.: Fear, Despair and Guns," *National Law Journal*, 18 April 1994, p. A1.

error. The report went on to state that 78 percent supported the continuation of the police reading suspects their Miranda rights.

It is reasonable to conclude from the survey data that the population of the United States, although fearful of the increase in criminal activity, along with its perception that the police and the criminal justice system cannot cope with crime sufficiently, are nonetheless loathe to sacrifice civil right guarantees that are now in place in order to enhance their personal safety. It is possible that the population has been "cultured" into the belief that the United States Constitution is unique to this country, and that the citizens are fortunate indeed to be inhabitants of the United States. Clearly, to change any Amendment would be an arduous task. If the population, seeing its "desperate need" to fight crime, would not be strong enough to sway public opinion, then the politicians would have small support to undertake such a far-reaching measure to attempt to cure the problem. Changing the "basic civil rights" of the American people through the political process of Congress, the President and state ratification appears remote. However, the Supreme Court has the ability to expand or limit protections by a five to four majority.

Polls and Surveys - England

The *Daily Telegraph* reported a study that was conducted for the Royal Commission on Criminal Justice.[21] This survey examined over one thousand cases from all over England. It determined that the use of the "right to silence" was significant in only five percent of the cases. With a conviction rate of fifty percent for these one thousand cases, the report concluded that the suspect's right to silence may have hampered conviction in two to three percent of the cases. Also examined was the relationship in acquittals and the suspect remaining silent. The findings showed that "while the defendant had been silent during interrogation in ten percent of such cases, the majority failed for reasons that were unconnected."[22] The report went on to conclude that abolishing the right to silence would have little impact on the cases. This study's report fails to provide survey structure data. One could assume from the report that, whether or not there is in place a right to remain silent, it makes or affords little protection. This conclusion on the part of the *Daily*

---

[21] "Study Backs the Right to Silence," *Daily Telegraph*, 2 February 1993, p. 6.
[22] Ibid.

Telegraph is based on its findings that the rate of conviction for those interrogated was similar to those not interrogated, and that other factors needed to be considered.

Another survey dealing with convictions based solely upon confessions cited attorney incompetence rather than right to silence as primary concerns.[23] This report also noted a survey by a *Solicitors Journal* which indicated continued support for the suspect to have the right to remain silent by 61 percent of those surveyed. The *Solicitors Journal* data fails to indicate the total number of those surveyed and the method of obtaining the polling data. Also absent are the respondents' classification for opposition to the right to silence, as well as those percentages of respondents who were undecided.

What is disturbing in the surveys reported by the various newspapers is that the newspapers report the changes in the "caution" being revised as an "abolition of the right to silence." With media incorrectly portraying this situation, it calls into question the manner in which the questions were constructed and the method of the various surveys themselves. The *Independent* of May 9, 1994 is a case in point.[24] How can one determine what the country thinks about a particular matter if the point in question is not identified properly? The abolition of a right is drastically different as compared to minor changes in the description of the right offered. Prior to the new "caution," the suspect could remain silent and request a lawyer. Subsequent to the passage by the House of Commons to include a warning to the suspect that the judge could note the suspect's silence to the jury does not deprive that suspect of his right to silence. Nor does it deprive him of his right to an attorney. Abolition of a right has not occurred. What has occurred is the implementation of the political agenda of the reporting paper, thereby biasing the perception to its readers as to what is involved.

This paper was instrumental in conducting a deliberative poll mentioned earlier. A cross-section of three hundred people was brought to one location for an intensive weekend of debate and discussion. Collaborating with the *Independent* was Channel 4. Values offered by those polled were "effective" or "very effective." The following is excerpted from the report published in the May 9, 1994 edition.[25]

---

[23] "Defence Lawyers Errors 'Ignored'," *Guardian*, 5 July 1993, p. 2.

[24] "Crime: What the Country Really Thinks," *Independent*, 9 May 1994, p. 9.

[25] Ibid. p. 1.

	Before	After
A - Do prison sentences lower crime?	57%	38%
B - Rights of Suspects to remain silent without it being held against them	57%	41%

Other reported results showed a marked increase to re-instate the death penalty but no numbers were reported.

With the biased reporting by the staff writer for the newspaper, the entire survey is brought into question as to its reliability, method of question formation and desired outcome for future action or non-action. As earlier noted, a deliberative poll conducted in an unbiased fashion is a proper sounding board against which to test ideas. If the survey is conducted by professionals careful to eliminate areas of bias in either the formation of the question or by careful selection of balanced interests in the debate panels, then an informed select group should provide safe guidance for future action. But the final analysis is still only opinion. The actual effects of such legislation upon crime and criminals can only be properly realized by empirical research such as the two studies performed by Paul Cassell.

Whereas perception of "rights" and the reality of "rights" are concerned, the perception is more to the short-term, while the reality is shaped in consequences over the long term. In politics, the memory of the voters appears to be, in some cases, of short duration. Unless the issue is passionately held, political positions on various issues can be modified over time. Herein could lie the danger in revising perceived rights. The surveys in England tend to illustrate that even the fear of crime does not lessen the population's perception of its protection from the excesses of government inquiry.

CHAPTER 8
CONCLUSION

The research has provided answers for some areas of concern but has also, perhaps, brought to the fore some new questions for consideration. If there are alternative methods to fact finding, how are they affected under each political/legal system of the United States and England?

It is obvious that, for the accused to be able to defend himself, there must be in place a method whereby the accused can remain silent and someone else speak in his defense. The old method "the accused speaks" provided for the accused to defend himself by answering question by question, refuting or denying, where possible, the charges or allegations now issuing from the bench. At the time when "the accused speaks" was in vogue, persons charged with serious crimes were not allowed the assistance of defense counsel. This situation precluded counsel for felonies but allowed for defense counsel in cases of misdemeanors, because many misdemeanors were concerned with civil actions. Blackstone wrote "For upon what face of reason can that assistance of counsel be denied to save the life of a man, which yet is allowed him in prosecutions for every petty trespass?"[1] Once it became accepted practice to have defense counsel, it became possible for the lawyer of the accused to question the case against his client. When lawyers for both the defense and prosecution controlled the proceedings, rather than just a judge, several new outcomes were realized. One, the prosecution was now under pressure to prove its case beyond a reasonable doubt. Second, the privilege against self-incrimination was solidly entrenched. The defendant, now having an attorney to defend him, no longer needed to be a witness. The courtroom procedure is now metamorphosed from where "the accused speaks" to "testing the case by the prosecution." Both of these conditions now prevail at trial, but where the jury or judge must determine if the

---

[1] *Commentaries on the Laws of England*, quoted in John H. Langbein, *Michigan Law Review 1994* 92 Mich. L. Rev. 1047 (1994): 63.

prosecution proved its case beyond a reasonable doubt, it is often determined long after the actual trial itself as to what might be self-incrimination.

If the progression of decisions relating to protecting the defendant is viewed over time, it becomes apparent that the period of 1960 to 1972, or thereabouts, reflects Supreme Court decisions in such a manner. Prior to the Warren Court, states' rights in matters at trial were, for the most part, not proper subjects to be reviewed. The Federal system, that is a separate Federal and state judicial system of procedures, was closer in concept to the original intent of the Framers in 1787, than it was to become. The Warren Court, perhaps looking to engineer social changes, used its judicial review powers to usurp power from the states and began to nullify the Federal system in favor of a de facto unitary one. The expansion and contraction of judicial powers now began in earnest.

The political agenda of the Democratic Party began to embrace social issues on a major scale, and this concern with social issues appears to have been in lock-step with the judicial decisions rendered at the time. If one were to analyze the recent decisions of the Supreme Court and compare those decisions with the English determination to curb crime, the final position reached would most likely be that in the United States the right of the accused to remain silent is a better protection than in England. However, this analysis must be viewed as part of a dynamic process subject to Supreme Court rulings and crime legislation geared to control criminal activity.

Is There an Alternative?

There has been, throughout the years, the effect of science impacting on the criminal justice system. The electronic media and freedom of speech is but one example of impingement upon the First Amendment. The Fourth Amendment has hosted a large array of modernization in society and the effects upon rights to privacy and search and seizure issues. The Eighth Amendment has confronted new methods of executions across the spectrum of time. With regard to the Fifth Amendment and in particular the "right to silence" there appears to be reluctance to come to grips with the issue. Defense lawyers cringe at any attempt to validate polygraph usage while, at the same time, espousing a dedicated commitment to "seek the truth." Yet defense lawyers overwhelmingly are the advocates of not wanting various types of evidence introduced at trial for any number of reasons. The seeking of truth can take many paths and, if justice and truth are the desired goals, why not allow all types to compete at trial, if they fulfill Frye requirements? But even Frye has given way to an expanded meaning allowing for the admission of evidence. In 1993 Daubert[2] allowed for competing viewpoints to be heard in court as to the reliability and validity of scientific techniques. The history of Frye is three quarters of a century long, providing guidance in many new areas of criminal investigation such as:

A. Forward looking radar systems[3]

B. Chromatographic analysis of ink[4]

C. Gunshot residue tests[5]

D. Voice prints[6]

E. Psychiatric testimony[7]

F. Blood splatter analysis[8]

G. Blood group typing[9]

H. Bitemark comparisons[10]

I. Microscopic comparisons of hair samples[11]

to name just the major examples.

In 1975 Congress enacted the Uniform Rules of Evidence. Rule 702 stated "If scientific, technical, or other specialized knowledge will assist the trier of fact to understand the evidence or determine a fact in issue, a witness qualified as an expert by knowledge, skill, experience, training, or education, may testify thereto in the form of an opinion or otherwise."

This new ruling set aside Frye and now allows a more liberal approach to the admission of evidence or testimony. The case of Daubert saw the Supreme Court unanimously holding that Frye was incompatible with the new Rule 702 and the

---

[2]Daubert v. Merrel Dow Pharmaceuticals, 113 S. Ct. 2786. (1993).

[3] United States v. Kilgus, 571 F. 2nd 508 (9th Cir. 1978).

[4] United States v. Bruno, 333 F. Supp. 570 (E.D. Pa. 1971).

[5] State v. Smith, 362 N.E. 2d 1239 (Ohio Ct. App. 1976).

[6] United States v. Addison, 498 F. 2d 741 (D.C. Cir. 1974).

[7] Hughes v. Mathews, 576 F. 2d 1250 (7th Cir.) Cert. Denied, 439 U.S. 801 (1978).

[8] Mustafa v. United States Parole Comm'n, 479 U.S. 953 (1986).

[9] Huntingdon v. Crowley, 414 P. 2d 382 (Cal. 1966).

[10] People v. Sloane, 143 Cal Rptr. 61 (Ct. App. 2d Dist. 1978).

[11] People v. Watkins, 259 N.W. 2d 381 (Mich. Ct. App. 1977).

relevancy standard. Since Daubert, all Federal courts and many state courts simply require that scientific evidence be relevant and reliable.

Enter now the polygraph. What could be more compelling than to be able to place before a judge or jury evidence that conclusively indicates the truth of a testimony? There has been widespread opposition to this method of fact finding by defense lawyers. Consider this. If there is a method of decisively indicating the truth of a matter, and the accused maintains his innocence, but does not avail himself to take a polygraph, the problem of the defense to create an aura of doubt is severely limited. Also, this method of fact finding makes our deepest secrets revealable to the world. This is frightening. But if this method can be so devastating, why is it not used more, and why is it not more acceptable across the spectrum? Argument has been successful in showing that the polygraph is not infallible. It is not one hundred percent accurate. There can be mistakes made, and possibly send an innocent suspect to prison. If this argument was used to challenge all other methods of determining evidence, what would survive? Are blood tests not also fallible? What about the comparison of fingerprints? ballistics? eye-witness testimony? And of considerable interest, the testimony of the accused, whose welfare is most in jeopardy at trial? There is a central paradox of the trial paradigm and this is the need for the reliable representation of facts. Such representations are commonly made by witnesses who may be less than truthful in their testimony. To combat this, our legal system attempts to utilize various safeguards to secure accuracy in testimony. Oaths and prosecution of perjurers are among the most noteworthy. With a polygraph, there are two possible outcomes in considering error rates. One is a false positive where the person is telling the truth and the second, a false negative, where deceit is not registered by the equipment. With the realization that no technology is without error, what is an acceptable rate of error for use of this information at trial? That there is serious regard in this matter is to recognize the prejudicial nature to the accused when the jury views such evidence. A polygraph's results may overshadow all other evidence in its effect upon the decision making process of the jury. Perhaps this is the proper role in which to view this technology. See table 6.

TABLE 6

VALIDITY OF EXAMINERS' DECISIONS
(inconclusives excluded)

Authors/Date	NDI			DI			Total			Technique
	# /	# Correct /	%	# /	# Correct /	%	# /	# Correct /	%	
Arellano (1990)	18	18	100%	22	22	100%	40	40	100%	Backster Zone
Edwards (1981)	363	356	98%	596	587	98%	959	943	98%	Variety
Elaad & Schahar (1985)	100	95	95%	74	73	99%	174	168	97%	Reid CQT & Backster Zone
Matte & Reuss (1989)	54	54	100%	60	60	100%	114	114	100%	Quadri-zone
Murray (1989)	21	18	86%	150	150	100%	171	168	98%	Arther CQT
Patrick & Iacono (1987)	30	27	90%	51	51	100%	81	78	96%	CQT
Putnam (1983)	65	62	95%	220	219	99%	285	281	99%	Backster Zone & MGQT
Raskin et al (1988)	28	27	96%	57	54	95%	85	81	95%	CQT
Widacki (1982)*	--	--	--	--	--	--	38	35	92%	Backster Zone
Yamamura & Miyake (1980)	65	61	94%	30	24	80%	95	85	89%	POT
TOTALS	744	718	97%	1260	1240	98%	2042	1993	98%	
TOTALS (less Edwards and Yamamura & Miyake)	316	301	95%	634	629	99%	988	965	98%	

Source: Norman Ansley, "The Validity and Reliability of Polygraph Decisions in Real Cases." Study prepared for the American Polygraph Association.

*Only the totals reported.

POT = Peak of Tension
CQT = Control Question tests
RI = Relevant/Irrelevant technique
DI = Deception indicated
NDI = No Deception indicated

Extensive experiments by Norman Ansley[12] show the accuracy rate for polygraphs to be in the range of eighty percent to one hundred percent. What is of significance is that more than one method of question formation was used. Included are the major studies of the previous ten years because they are representative of current trends.

Results:

Not all tests invoked control questions and some tests may have employed various types. Of the Control Question Tests (QCT), excluding Edwards and Yamamura, examiners were correct in 301 out of 316 No Deception Indicated (NDI) for a 95 percent rate. They were correct in 629 out of 634 Deception Indicated (DI) for 99 percent. Unlike Peak Of Tensions (POT), the control question tests were more accurate with guilty subjects. If Edwards is included the No Deception Indicated numbers are 656 of 679 for a 96 percent rate. The Deception Indicated rate was 99 percent obtained from 1,216 of 1,230 cases. The ground truth against which these percentages were obtained included either the confession of the accused or a "charge partner" of the accused or upon court decisions. Also included were follow-ups based upon both, and some had the addition of physical evidence. There are two weaknesses that should be noted. Physical evidence and court decisions are unreliable. Confessions are better as false confessions are rare, but the researcher must be mindful that the types of individuals who will confess are a different breed from those who refuse, and deception detection between those groups may not truly reflect the accuracy of such detection.

Other studies show singular techniques and concern themselves with isolated portions of the craft. This study was selected because of its "real world" content and its inclusive use of all major indicators. The first table addressed validity, the next table will provide the reliability analysis. This measurement is a blind analysis where the evaluator does not know the facts of the case. This study assumed that the blind evaluators and examiners were of comparable levels of competency and that all had similar amounts of experience. Other concerns addressed the background of the scorers, as there are different schools of polygraph utilizing different methods of scoring the charts. So the scoring methods and the scoring of others' charts were of some concern. Another notable point was the detail of the chart markings, and

---

[12] Norman Ansley, "The Validity and Reliability of Polygraph Decisions in Real Cases." Study prepared for the American Polygraph Association.

whether or not the evaluator used any assumptions in his markings. The results of Table 7 indicated correction rates from 83 percent and greater -- significantly greater than chance. If we accept these results as valid, and there do not appear to be results to the contrary, the criminal justice system faces a dilemma of two parts. First, how to gain court approval for the introduction of polygraph results in all criminal cases, and second, combatting constitutional concerns.

Such concerns address:

A.   Is it still appropriate to allow the accused to remain silent when there is technology for determining truth

B.   Should the courts/Constitution protect the accused or allow the Government to establish the accused's guilt

C.   The Fifth Amendment may have failed to predict this set of circumstances

One possible solution would be Congressional hearings assessing the technology that pits science against law.

One possible solution would allow for a more liberal use of the polygraph in civil proceedings. Another would, in criminal cases, allow the accused to enter a polygraph result to prove innocence, while providing that the prosecution would need more than just a polygraph test to secure a conviction. Other points to consider would be a re-vamping of the trial itself from that of an accusatorial nature to the inquisition model where the judge is the seeker of truth. This would still allow for cross-examination between opposing sides. This would model those countries using a civil law basis for their proceedings. This method is used in the majority of countries. If truth is what is desired, obtaining it in the face of scientific advances clearly invades areas protected presently by Constitutional directive. The Constitution of the United States and its attendant Bill of Rights has been hailed for its ability to adapt to changing times. The rapid advancement of science may be posing, to this Constitution, the strongest challenges yet.

The research therefore shows that a suspect's "right to silence" is better protected under the United States system with its written Constitution and the Bill of Rights limiting the Government's actions against the individual. The cases brought before the Supreme Court praying for relief because of unique circumstances, real or imagined, demonstrate a commitment over time to provide protection to the accused.

TABLE 7

RELIABILITY OF BLIND CHART ANALYSIS
(inconclusives excluded)

Authors/Date	NDI #	# Correct	%	DI #	# Correct	%	Total #	# Correct	%	Technique
Arellano (1990)	18	18	100%	22	22	100%	40	40	100%	Backster Zone (numerical scoring)
Elaad (1985)	30	23	77%	30	23	77%	60	46	77%	CQT (numerical scoring)
Elaad (1985)	30	27	90%	30	23	77%	60	50	83%	CQT (global scoring)
Franz (1989)	49	33	67%	50	47	94%	99	83	84%	Reid CQT (numerical scoring)
Honts & Driscoll (1988)*	--	--	--	--	--	--	52	46	88%	CWT (numerical scoring)
Honts & Raskin (1988)	10	8	80%	11	11	100%	21	19	90%	Utah Zone, less one control (DL) (numerical scoring)
Jayne (1990)*	--	--	--	--	--	--	100	92	92%	Reid CQT (numerical scoring)
Matte & Reuss (1989)	54	54	100%	60	60	100%	114	114	100%	Quadri-Zone (numerical scoring)
Patrick & Iacono (1987)	20	11	55%	49	48	98%	69	59	86%	Canadian CQT (numerical scoring)
Raskin et al (1988)	22	19	86%	48	45	94%	70	64	91%	CQT (numerical scoring)
Ryan (1989)*	--	--	--	--	--	--	255	218	85%	Reid CQT (numerical scoring)
TOTALS	233	193	83%	300	279	93%	940	831	88%	

Source: Norman Ansley, "The Validity and Reliability of Polygraph Decisions in Real Cases." Study prepared for the American Polygraph Association.

*Only the totals reported

That the protection could be expanded is still a player in the arena. It is conceivable that a Supreme Court could view the Fifth Amendment in the same legal light as the state courts, prior to *Weeks*. This viewpoint allows for the rapid expansion of protections originally considered by the state courts. Again, all that would be required is a ruling/interpretation of the Fifth Amendment protections, disregarding Wigmore's position as to what is considered testimony, as discussed earlier in the research. The withdrawing of body fluids appears to circumvent the protection against one being a "compelled" entity to provide evidence, but if the intent of the originators of the Bill of Rights is considered in context with the level of investigative procedures in place at that time, then the strict interpretation of the Fifth Amendment is proper. Clouding this issue somewhat have been the pronouncements of the Court however, to "broaden protections of other rights" provided in the accompanying Amendments. Whereas there has been a narrowing of the protection, as witnessed by the cases indicated from the late nineteenth century to Miranda of the twentieth century, the "compelling" of testimony by force has been, for the most part, eliminated. If one agrees with Wigmore that only testimony is protected, then interrogation prior to trial is not included. The procedure for change in the Amendment, absent Supreme Court unilateral decisions, is a long and arduous one. Extensive debate in both houses of Congress would necessarily ensue if a change in the Amendment was pondered. This is highly unlikely, witness the Equal Rights Amendment of the late 1970s. Ratification of this Amendment, which endangered no one nor placed anyone in jeopardy of incarceration, was defeated through failing to get the requisite three-quarters of states' legislatures to ratify; this after being accepted by two-thirds vote of both houses in Congress. Amending anything by this method, in the Bill of Rights, would almost certainly fail as well. The Supreme Court, as mentioned earlier, could expand the Federal viewpoint to encompass the earlier protection granted by the state courts in the late 1800s. Given the social damage reported in Cassell's reports, this appears most unlikely as well. For, if Miranda could have a negative impact on conviction rates, the widening of the umbrella of protections granted in the Fifth Amendment would increase the level of alarm in the population and, quite possibly, bring about "vigilante" actions at worse, or increased political replacement of legislatures at best. Recent political dialogue in Congress has voiced desires to fully implement the Tenth Amendment, which would return to the states those rights not ceded to the Federal Government. How the resurrection of the Tenth Amendment would affect decisions based upon the Fourteenth Amendment is yet to be decided. If the states retain certain rights, and the Fourteenth Amendment abrogates those rights, it is possible to see a case being made for revising the Fourteenth Amendment or having it declared unconstitutional. There are definite, serious constitutional issues that need to be addressed in order to provide equal Amendment protection from *all* of the amendments based upon the provisions of the Bill of Rights. Some previous Supreme Court decisions may clearly reside outside the scope of the Federal Government because of the nature of the Federal system at hand. The Founding Fathers clearly wanted a limitation upon Federal authority insinuating itself into the workings of the state. With this in mind, state trials may revert to having various degrees of protections for the accused, as witnessed by the state cases prior to Weeks. It is not reasonable to expect a serious erosion of the right to remain silent as this right was broader under state control, it having been narrowed by the action of the Supreme Court as illustrated earlier in the research.

> James Madison believed that the greatest threat to human rights in a popular government is the majority tyranny that results when one faction seizes control of the entire power of government and uses it to advance its own selfish interests at the expense of all other interests.[13]

This viewpoint of Madison allows for competing interests in the country to exist, but with the Federal Government wielding the power through the Fourteenth Amendment, we move from a heterogeneous society to a homogenized one. Almond contends that "a political culture is a particular distribution of political attitudes, values, feelings, information, and skills."[14] This political culture in the United States provides a basis for most Americans thinking highly of themselves as Americans while somewhat cautious in their views of their politicians. It is with this in mind that Americans most value *their* Bill of Rights. Americans have been socialized to value highly the United States Constitution, perhaps more so than other populations

---

[13] Gabriel A. Almond and G. Bingham Powell, Jr., gen. eds. *Comparative Politics Today: A World View*, 5th ed. (New York: HarperCollins Publishers, 1992), p. 567.

[14] Ibid. p. 569.

and their laws and governments. George Washington remarked on the uniqueness of the United States in his inaugural address, saying,

> The preservation of the sacred fire of liberty, and the destiny of the republican model of government, are justly considered as deeply, perhaps as finally staked, on the experiment entrusted to the hands of the American people.[15]

It is therefore no wonder that Americans cherish their "rights." However, "rights" do not come without responsibility. The mere fact that someone has "rights" does not remove obligations that are co-committant with those "rights." It is a zero sum situation. The individual exercises his right to silence which is not absolute, witness the immunities discussed earlier. There are rights to free speech and freedom of expression, but a restaurant which had a sign saying "No handicapped people" would find itself afoul the Federal law, thus modifying rights of speech, freedom of expression, right to assembly, etc. That the United States Supreme Court issued decisions on all variances of free speech, it is not likely that the right to silence would be so abridged even if scientific progress allowed for it. If our thoughts and secrets are to be laid bare through effective scientific apparatuses, then political freedom is also jeopardized. For, if the "self" is not held inviolate, then neither can the accumulation of "selves" be so. Intrusions of a moderate nature are now tolerated by society recognizing that the needs of society are being carefully balanced against the "rights" of the individual, but the operative word is "balanced."

It is therefore concluded that each Amendment has the potential to have its protections extended or diminished at the discretion of the Supreme Court. However, it is also of note that a written Bill of Rights, wherein each right is formidable in its own protections, when these rights are interwoven, can constitute a legal fabric in which the citizen can clothe himself with a substantial degree of security. This protection allows for a population to have real impact on the political process without undue fear of reprisal. With societies in competition for various resources, this political trust can be maneuvered to obtain the items of priority for that particular group. Absent this political trust, the population would seek out ways to effect what it considers to be needed adjustments outside those afforded by the orderly process

---

[15] Ibid. p. 595.

of laws and balloting. To be considered are even those who are unsuccessful in their initial attempts to secure their goals. Political and legal history in the United States has demonstrated that the protection of minorities does, in fact, take place, and the opposition of those minorities to various in-place institutions can be coerced to modify their alienating actions. The civil rights movement of the 1960s provides emphatic proof that this is true.

In England the process to further limit the right to silence passed the new regulations with minor difficulties. Moreover, the new regulations, having been passed by Parliament are not subject to additional review for legitimization. The recent cry in England for a written Bill of Rights underscores the importance such a document demands.

The clash of science with the legal system is not yet over; rather, it has just begun. If the original intent of the right to silence was predicated upon the use of torture to secure the truth, it is reasonable to assume that increases in crime, coupled with advances in science, may create an atmosphere wherein the right to silence becomes the duty to speak. The Bill of Rights has shielded the citizens of the United States for over two hundred years. The next fifty years may be the most crucial to its survival.

The paucity of English cases demonstrates that the legal aspects of protecting its citizens are not as often challenged as in the United States. The English courts are more closely focused as to legal issues considered to be heard. The judicial review in the United States considers issues of legal procedure within the criminal justice system, as well as issues regarding the constitutionality of the law itself. The issue of legality of the law is absent in England as this is outside the scope of authority of its judicial appellate process. The options for challenge by the accused are therefore somewhat limited in England whereas, in the United States, the limitations are only a function of limited legal imagination of the defense team. That imagination has provided for the Supreme Court decisions emphatically voiced in the First Amendment's decisions. Further, whereas there are court recognitions of Multiple Personality Disorder variances, the English courts do not address this issue at all. This cannot be for lack of legal imagination on the part of the barristers or solicitors engaged in defense tactics.

The use of the polygraph is conspicuously absent in England also. Usage of this technology appears to be limited, and court cases based upon its use are limited as well, to its use by the Government in areas of espionage.

The Framers of the United States Constitution were more concerned with property issues and political concerns interfering with trade as opposed to issues of crime and criminal procedure. This original intent of the Bill of Rights, to offer political protection, assumed as a secondary area of concern criminal accusations of all types. This adoption by the Bill of Rights speaks well for its versatility.

With these points in mind, further support is given to the contention that a written Bill of Rights clearly outlining protections, and with the mechanism to change these rights long and arduous, provides a substantial legal foundation upon which the citizens can rely for protection. The judicial review provided for under the United States Constitution allows for minor expansion and contraction of legal guarantees, without the necessity for wholesale overhaul because of changing conditions. It has been demonstrated that the United States' approach to judicial review is two-fold: one being the review of judicial outcomes of trial courts, and the second by the Supreme Court in its role of overseeing the laws generated by Congress.

A comparison between the United States and England of outcomes at trials is difficult because of the underlying protections of the Bill of Rights enjoyed by the accused in the United States. In England, for instance, there is no exclusionary rule, as all evidence is admissible regardless of the manner in which it was obtained. So, for someone to remark that in England elimination of confessions would have little impact on convictions would at first appear meaningful. But this must be viewed within the entire framework of the English system. Would the United States' population be willing to trade some protections by enhancing selected ones and eliminating others? It may very well be that the protections of the accused's right to silence are but "keystones" to an arch that embraces all covered by its strength.

Consider the following. At trial, the presence of a suspect's fingerprints (or other physical evidence) at the scene of a crime is evidence against the accused. However, *lack* of such evidence is usually noted by the defense to support the contention that the accused is innocent. If we follow this line of logic of evidence/no evidence, then the accused's failure to testify, denying such accusations, should also be allowed by the prosecution. The accused is not compelled to testify to provide incriminating statements, but how can the denial of wrongdoing, by an innocent person, be harmful? A court of law is the place in which the search for truth takes place. No torture is presumed. No fear, other than what is appropriate under the circumstance, is induced. That anyone taking an oath or affirmation feels apprehensive is a normal occurrence for those who do not testify as a matter of course in daily life. The court can compel an accused to give intimate samples but shrinks from placing the accused on the stand to deny accusations of guilt! Perhaps what has occurred is Maslow's hierarchy of needs being applied to legal issues. Maslow's pinnacle of achievement, that of "self-actualization" appears to come into play. The lofty ideals of justice have set up unrealistic rules to combat crime. Those who are engaged in crime do not follow those rules. It is as if we have one side playing baseball while the other is engaged in soccer. It may be well to note that crime detection and criminal activity may not have been the focus of the Bill of Rights but rather political protection from Government. If this is so, how then would it alter the criminal justice system of the United States? This thought bears weight, because organized police activity did not occur until some fifty years after the Bill of Rights.

If the Bill of Rights was introduced because of criminal activity, is it not also plausible to assume that some mechanisms, as a part of government, would have been in place to combat crime? The excesses of the English monarchy upon the colonists were those oppressions of a political/economic nature having more to do with politics and trade rather than crimes against people. Property crime was influential in the drafting of the Constitution, and property was safeguarded by its dictates, but again, the underlying purpose was protection *from* Government.

If a newly emerging country wishes to duplicate the system of law in England, it would be adequate if there has been enough time for that country to build a foundation of trust over time that allows for a legal expectation to exist wherein the rights of the accused are accepted on a cultural level and imbedded into the country's tradition. However, absent this long legal history, it appears the United States model would be better suited in providing real and long-term protection to that country's citizens.

Outbreaks of crime, or severe increases in criminal activity do not place the general population in jeopardy, witness the use of intrusive wire-taps and organized crime. If there is to be a danger to the Bill of Rights, that danger will come from the area from which the original protection emanated -- economic concerns. Economic concerns have the face of Government on them, and it is that face the population will see if economic prosperity is no longer a reality. The Government may have to act in such a fashion that the Bill of Rights, which is guaranteed by the Government, may be set aside to effect control of a population that is disenchanted with the economic outlook and realities.

A written Constitution is a constant reminder to both the people and the Government of the political contract that exists between them. The written word becomes part of the political expectations of the people and it is incorporated into its culture. It becomes referred to on a day-to-day basis, and children are informed of its value at an early age in their education. In short, the population "internalizes" the Constitution and its protections, especially if it has served them well for over two hundred years. To attempt any change in the protections provided would cause alarm and concern in the people, even if the touted reasons for the change were serious in nature. As stated earlier, the different competing demographic groups would all consider such changes in relationship as to how they themselves would be affected. Rarely, if ever, could such an undertaking be viewed without a considerable degree of suspicion and distrust. The polling data also indicated that the population was willing to concede "Exclusionary Rule" protection while it was less eager to relinquish "Miranda" protections.[16] This is most likely a by-product of the people realizing that they can be searched against their will provided certain criteria are maintained, and any evidence properly obtained can be used against them. The right to silence offers protection even if it is circumvented by the various grants of immunity, for then the evidence obtained through such a grant of immunity is prohibited for the prosecution of the accused.

In the final analysis, it is determined that the protection afforded under the system in the United States is superior to the English protection because of two facts. First, the protection is codified in a written Bill of Rights and, second, the process to

---

[16] "Ohioans Support Suspects' Constitutional Rights," *Regional News* (Cincinnati), 28 July, 1987. p. B4.

alter this document is a long procedure with many safeguards available. Although the United States Supreme Court can set aside the provisions of protection, the Supreme Court cannot alter the basic document. This provides underlying protection allowing for minor changes by the Supreme Court. Even if the Supreme Court were to rule major changes in the protection granted, the Supreme Court cannot effect a major change in the Bill of Rights that would be viable for a significant period of time. To restate the English position, a new law by Parliament would eliminate, or create, a new doctrine in but a single step.

APPENDIX 1
THE USE OF IMMUNITY

A state or the federal government is not obligated to plea-bargain or grant immunity. But it is sometimes necessary in order to obtain the evidence and witnesses needed to obtain a criminal conviction in a court.

Pocket Immunity

Immunity is a promise not to prosecute for the named crime in return for the cooperation of the person in the manner agreed upon in the immunity agreement. The immunity granted could be "pocket immunity," which was described by the Sixth Circuit in the 1991 case of *Turner v. United States*, 936 F. 2d 221, 223, as:

... This informal immunity arises by way of assurances by prosecutors, either orally or by letter, to a potential grand jury witness that he will be immune from any prosecution based upon that testimony. Such decisions are made informally, outside the supervision of a court. The legality of granting informal immunity has been upheld in a number of circuits. ...

... Pocket immunity is nothing more than a promise on the part of the prosecutor that they would not be charged in that district and that their testimony would not be disseminated to other government agencies. Such promises of "immunity" are contractual in nature and do not bind other parties not privy to the original agreement.

Federal Statutory Immunity

The Sixth Federal Circuit Court of Appeals described federal statutory immunity as follows in 1991:

... The federal immunity statute prohibits the compelled testimony of a witness from being used against him "in any criminal case...." Immunity of Witnesses Act, para. 201(a), 18 U.S.C. para. para. 6001-6005. In order for a federal prosecutor to grant this type of immunity, he must receive approval from both the United States Attorney in the relevant judicial district, and from a high-ranking official in the Justice Department; the immunity grant must also be approved by a federal district judge. See 18 U.S.C. para. 6003. This immunity assures a witness that his immunized testimony will be inadmissible in any future criminal proceeding, as will be any evidence obtained by prosecutors directly or indirectly as a result of the immunized testimony. 18 U.S.C. para 6002.

In *Kastigar v. United States*, 406 U.S. 441, 92 S.Ct. 1653, 32 L. Ed. 2d 212 (1972), the Supreme Court held that when a witness who has given incriminating testimony under a grant of immunity pursuant to 18 U.S.C. para 6002 is subsequently prosecuted for a matter related to the compelled testimony, the government bears "the heavy burden of proving that all of the evidence it proposes to use was derived from legitimate independent sources." *Id.* at 461, 92 S.Ct. at 1665. See also *Murphy v. Waterfront Comm'n of New York*, 378 U.S. 52, 84 S.Ct. 1594, 12 L. Ed. 2d 678 (1964). 936 F. 2d at 223.

Compelled or Forced Testimony

Legislative bodies (the U.S. Congress and state legislatures) have the power to grant immunity, as do federal and state prosecutors. In most instances, witnesses receiving immunity voluntarily enter into an immunity agreement.

Source: Thomas J. Gardner and Terry M. Anderson, *Criminal Evidence: Principles and Cases* 3rd ed. (Minneapolis/St. Paul: West Publishing Company, 1988), Introduction.

APPENDIX 2
THE PRIVILEGE AGAINST SELF-INCRIMINATION

The Fifth Amendment to the United States Constitution, ratified in 1791, states "No person . . . shall be compelled in any criminal case to be a witness against himself. . . ." In tracing the origins and roots of the Fifth Amendment's right to remain silent, the United States Supreme Court pointed out in the case of *Miranda v. Arizona* that the privilege's "roots go back into ancient times," and probably has origins in the Bible.

The Fifth Amendment's privilege against self-incrimination is the only privilege given constitutional protection. All other privileges exist only by statutory or common law. In 1896, the United States Supreme Court pointed this out in the case of *Brown v. Walker*, 161 U.S. 591, 597, 16 S.Ct. 644, 647.

The privilege "protects a person . . . against being incriminated by his own compelled testimonial communications." *Fisher v. United States* 425 U.S. 391, 409, 96 S.Ct. 1569,1580 (1976). Because statements made by a person in any civil hearing or questioning might later be used against that person in a criminal proceeding, the United States Supreme Court has repeatedly held that the privilege "can be asserted in any proceeding, civil or criminal, administrative or judicial, investigatory or adjudicatory." *Kastigar v. United States*, 406 U.S. 441, 444, 92 S.Ct. 1653, 1656 (1972). The privilege has thus been invoked, for example, in divorce and tax cases as well as in criminal cases and questioning by law enforcement officers.

The United States Supreme Court has held that the privilege against self-incrimination "reflects many of our fundamental values and noble aspirations." *Murphy v. Waterfront Comm.*, 378 U.S. 52, 55, 84 S.Ct. at 1594, 1596 (1964). Because it is "the essential mainstay of our adversary system," the United States Constitution requires "that the government seeking to punish an individual produce the evidence against him by its own independent labor rather than by the cruel, simple expedient of compelling it from his own mouth." *Miranda v. Arizona*, 384 U.S. 436, 460, 86 S.Ct. at 1602, 1620 (1966).

148

Immunity and the Privilege Against
Self-Incrimination

Under state and Federal statutes, prosecutors and legislative bodies may grant immunity to witnesses in order to encourage or compel the witness to testify. The grant of immunity means the witness can no longer be charged with the crime for which the immunity is granted, eliminating the possibility of incrimination and the need for Fifth Amendment privilege of protection against self-incrimination.

Statutes that Grant Immunity

In some areas state or Federal governments grant immunity by statute. For example, several states create a statutory privilege for statements made to a police officer after a motor vehicle accident has occurred.

Source: Thomas J. Gardner and Terry M. Anderson, *Criminal Evidence: Principles and Cases* 3rd ed. (Minneapolis/St. Paul: West Publishing Company, 1988), Introduction.

APPENDIX 3
AREAS WHERE FIFTH AMENDMENT PRIVILEGE AGAINST SELF-INCRIMINATION DOES NOT APPLY

The Fifth Amendment privilege against self-incrimination applies only to evidence of a communicative or testimonial nature. It does not apply when only physical evidence is sought and obtained. Seizure of physical evidence is controlled by the Fourth Amendment to the United States Constitution. Thus, the privilege against self-incrimination does not apply in the following circumstances:

A. A witness could testify that the defendant was compelled to put on a shirt and it fit him. *Holt v. United States*, 218 U.S. 245, 31 S.Ct. 2 (1910). (Would apply to any clothing or hat.)

B. The withdrawal of blood and use as evidence to show the defendant was driving while intoxicated at the time of accident was approved by the United States Supreme Court in *Schmerber v. California*, 384 U.S. 757, 86 S.Ct. 1826 (1966).

C. The use of a handwriting exemplar, or sample, was held to be controlled by the Fourth Amendment by the United States Supreme Court in *Gilber v. California*, 388 U.S. 263 87 S.Ct. 1951 (1967).

D. Compelling the accused to exhibit his person for observation, as in a lineup or showup. *United States v. Wade*, 388 U.S. 218, 87 S.Ct. 1926 (1967).

E. To make a voice exemplar, or sample. *United States v. Dionisio*, 410 U.S. 1, 93 S.Ct. 764 (1973).

F. Federal Courts of Appeal have held that no Fifth Amendment violation occurred where the defendant was compelled to wear a false goatee, *United States v. Hammond*, 419 F. 2d 166, 168 (4th Cir. 1969), cert. denied, 397 U.S. 1068, 90 S.Ct. 1508 (1970); to wear a wig, *United States v. Murray*, 523 F. 2d 489, 492 (8th Cir. 1975); to shave for identification purposes, *United States v. Valenzuela*, 722 F. 2d 1431, 1433 (9th Cir. 1983); to put on a stocking mask at trial to permit a witness to testify as to similarity to the masked robber, *United*

150

States v. Roberts, 481 F. 2d 892 (5th Cir. 1973); or to dye her or his hair to the color it was at the time of the offense, *United States v. Brown*, 920 F. 2d 1212 (5th Cir. 1991).

G. To corporations and organizations (the Fifth Amendment applies to persons only). *George Campbell Painting Corp. v. Reid*, 392 U.S. 286, 88 S. Ct. 1978 (1968); *United States v. Doe*, 465 U.S. 605, 104 S.Ct. 1237 (1984); *United States v. White* 322 U.S. 694, 64 S.Ct. 1248 (1944), held that an unincorporated union did not have the privilege against self-incrimination.

H. To records required for the benefit of the public, or records subject to public inspection. In *Shapiro v. United States*, 335 U.S. 1, 68 S.Ct. 1375 (1948), the records were required by law of transactions subject to government regulation.

I. Where immunity has been granted and the person is compelled to testify or agrees to testify as part of a plea agreement.

J. Where the incrimination is of others and is not self-incrimination. *Bursey v. United States*, 466 F. 2d 1059 (9th Cir. 1972).

K. Where the public interest in protecting children from abuse outweighs Fifth Amendment privilege. After a small child had received numerous physical injuries and the child's mother was seen abusing the child, the mother was ordered to disclose the location of the child. The mother was jailed on contempt when she would not do so. The United States Supreme Court affirmed the contempt sentence in *Baltimore Department of Social Services v. Bouknight*, 493 U.S. 549, 110 S.Ct. 900 (1990).

L. Where military service person failed to report drug use of other service personnel and was convicted of dereliction of duty. Defense that other personnel might retaliate and report Medley failed. *United States v. Medley*, 33 M.J. 75 (1991), review denied United States Supreme Court, U.S., 112 S. Ct. 1473, 50 CrL 3199 (1992). The Fifth Amendment privilege would apply had the service person been a party to the crime of drug use. *United States v. Heyward*, 22 M.J. 35 (C.M.A. 1986).

M. Where there has been a voluntary, intelligent waiver of the privilege.

Source: Thomas J. Gardner and Terry M. Anderson, *Criminal Evidence: Principles and Cases* 3rd ed. (Minneapolis/St. Paul: West Publishing Company, 1988), Introduction.

APPENDIX 4
ENGLAND - SELF INCRIMINATION

A.   In any proceedings in which a court is hearing an application for an order under Part IV or V, no person shall be excused from:

1.   giving evidence on any matter; or

2.   answering any question put to him in the course of his giving evidence on the ground that doing so might incriminate him or his spouse of an offence.

B.   A statement or admission made in such proceedings shall not be admissible in evidence against the person making it or his spouse in proceedings for an offence other than perjury.

Source: *Children Act 1989 (c41)*, Part XII Miscellaneous and General: Jurisdiction and Procedure, etc., Section: 98 Self-Incrimination. 16 November 1989.

APPENDIX 5

ENGLAND - WITHDRAWAL OF PRIVILEGE AGAINST INCRIMINATION OF SELF OR SPOUSE IN CERTAIN PROCEEDINGS

A. In any proceedings to which this subsection applies a person shall not be excused, by reason that to do so would tend to expose that person, or his or her spouse, to proceedings for a related offence or for the recovery of a related penalty:

   1. from answering any question put to that person in the first-mentioned proceedings; or

   2. from complying with any order made in those proceedings

B. Subsection (A) applies to the following civil proceedings in the High Court, namely:

   1. proceedings for infringement of rights pertaining to any intellectual property or for passing off

   2. proceedings brought to obtain disclosure of information relating to any infringement of such rights or to any passing off; and

   3. proceedings brought to prevent any apprehended infringement of such rights or any apprehended passing off

C. Subject to subsection (D), no statement or admission made by a person:

   1. in answering a question put to him in any proceedings to which subsection (A) applies; or

   2. in complying with any order made in any such proceedings

   shall, in proceedings for any related offence or for the recovery of any related penalty, be admissible in evidence against that person or (unless they married after the making of the statement or admission) against the spouse of that person.

D. Nothing in subsection (C) shall render any statement or admission made by a person as there mentioned inadmissible in evidence against that person in proceedings for perjury or contempt of court.

154

E.   In this section

"intellectual property" means any patent, trade mark, copyright (design right), registered design, technical or commercial information or other intellectual property;

"related offence" in relation to any proceedings to which subsection (A) applies, means:

1.   in the case of proceedings within subsection (B)(1) or (2)

   a)   any offence committed by or in the course of the infringement or passing off to which those proceedings relate; or

   b)   any offence not within sub-paragraph (a) committed in connection with that infringement or passing off, being an offence involving fraud or dishonesty

2.   in the case of proceedings within subsection (B)(3), any offence revealed by the facts on which the plaintiff relies in those proceedings;

"related penalty," in relation to any proceedings to which subsection (A) applies means:

1.   in the case of proceedings within subsection (B) (1) or (2), any penalty incurred in respect of anything done or omitted in connection with the infringement or passing off to which those proceedings relate

2)   in the case of proceedings within subsection (B) (3), any penalty incurred in respect of any act or omission revealed by the facts on which the plaintiff relies in those proceedings.

F.   Any reference in this section to civil proceedings in the High Court of any description includes a reference to proceedings on appeal arising out of civil proceedings in the High Court of that description.

Source: *Supreme Court Act 1981 (c54)*. Part III Practice and Procedure: The High Court: Other Provisions, Section: 72 Withdrawal of Privilege against Incrimination of Self or Spouse in Certain Proceedings. 18 July 1981.

APPENDIX 6

ENGLAND - PRIVILEGE AGAINST INCRIMINATION OF SELF OR SPOUSE IN CERTAIN PROCEEDINGS

A. The right of a person in any legal proceedings other than criminal proceedings to refuse to answer any question or produce any document or thing if to do so would tend to expose that person to proceedings for an offence or for the recovery of a penalty:

1. shall apply only as regards criminal offences under the law of any part of the United Kingdom and penalties provided for by such law; and

2. shall include a like right to refuse to answer any question or produce any document or thing if to do so would tend to expose the husband or wife of that person to proceedings for any such criminal offence or for the recovery of any such penalty.

B. In so far as any existing enactment conferring (in whatever words) powers of inspection or investigation confers on a person (in whatever words) any right otherwise than in criminal proceedings to refuse to answer any question or give any evidence tending to incriminate that person, subsection (A) above shall apply to that right as it applies to the right described in that subsection; and every such existing enactment shall be construed accordingly.

C. In so far as any existing enactment provides (in whatever words) that in any proceedings other than criminal proceedings a person shall not be excused from answering any question or giving any evidence on the ground that to do so may incriminate that person, that enactment shall be construed as providing also that in such proceedings a person shall not be excused from answering any question or giving any evidence on the ground that to do so may incriminate the husband or wife of that person.

D. Where any existing enactment (however worded) that:

1. confers powers of inspection or investigation; or

2. provides as mentioned in subsection (C) above,

further provides (in whatever words) that any answer or evidence given by a person shall not be admissible in evidence against that person in any proceedings or class of proceedings (however described, and whether criminal or not), that enactment shall be construed as providing also that any answer or evidence given by that person shall not be admissible in evidence against the husband or wife of that person in the proceedings or class of proceedings in question.

E. In this section "existing enactment" means any enactment passed before this Act; and the references to giving evidence are references to giving evidence in any manner, whether by furnishing information, making discovery, producing documents or otherwise.

Source: *Civil Evidence Act 1968 (c64)*. Part II Miscellaneous and General: Privilege, Section: 14 Privilege against Incrimination of Self or Spouse. 25 October 1968.

BIBLIOGRAPHY

BOOKS

Allen, Ronald J., and Kuhns, Richard B. Constitutional Criminal Procedure: An Examination of the Fourth, Fifth, and Sixth Amendments and Related Areas. 2nd ed. Boston: Little, Brown and Company, 1991.

Almond, Gabriel A., and Powell, G. Bingham, Jr. gen. eds. Comparative Politics Today: A World View 5th ed. New York: HarperCollins Publishers, 1992.

American Psychiatric Association. Diagnostic and Statistic Manual of Mental Disorders. 3rd ed. rev. Washington, DC: American Psychiatric Association, 1987.

Anderson, Terence, and Twining, William. Analysis of Evidence: How to Do Things with Facts Based on Wigmore's "Science of Judicial Proof". Boston: Little, Brown and Company, 1991.

Bacon, Francis, Sir. The Elements of the Common Lawes of England. London: Assignes of I. More Esq. 1630; reprint ed. New York: Da Capo Press, 1969.

Baker, J.H. An Introduction to English Legal History. 2nd ed. London: Butterworth, 1979.

Bartol, Curt R. Psychology and American Law. Belmont, CA: Wadsworth Publishing Company, 1983.

Bertsch, Gary K.; Clark, Robert P.; and Wood, David M. Comparing Political Systems: Power and Policy in Three Worlds. 4th ed. New York: Macmillan Publishing Company, 1991.

Bill, James A., and Hardgrave, Robert L. Jr. Comparative Politics: The Quest for Theory. Merrill Political Science Series. Columbus, OH: Charles E. Merrill Publishing Company, 1973.

Billias, George Athan, ed. Law and Authority in Colonial America: Selected Essays. Barre, MA: Barre Publishers, 1965.

Black, Henry Campbell. Black's Law Dictionary. 6th ed. St. Paul, MN: West Publishing Co., 1990.

158

Bodenhamer, David J. Fair Trial: Rights of the Accused in American History. New York and Oxford, UK: Oxford University Press, 1992.

Bracton. Bracton on the Laws and Customs of England. Translated by Samuel E. Thorne, vol. I. Cambridge, MA: The Belknap Press of Harvard University Press, 1968.

_____. Bracton on the Laws and Customs of England. Translated by Samuel E. Thorne, vol. 2. Cambridge, MA: The Belknap Press of Harvard University Press, 1968.

Brant, Irving. The Bill of Rights: Its Origin and Meaning. Indianapolis: Bobbs-Merrill, 1965.

Brown, C.R.; Maxwell, P.A.; and Maxwell L.F. comps. Canadian and British-American Colonial Law: From Earliest Times to December, 1956. London: Sweet & Maxwell, 1957.

Bryson, William Hamilton. Census of Law Books in Colonial Virginia. Charlottesville: University Press of Virginia, 1978.

Burton, Steven J. An Introduction to Law and Legal Reasoning. Boston: Little, Brown and Company, 1985.

Caenegem, R.C. van. The Birth of the English Common Law. 2nd ed. Cambridge: Cambridge University Press, 1988.

Calvi, James V., and Coleman, Susan. American Law and Legal Systems. 2nd ed. Englewood Cliffs, NJ: Prentice Hall, 1992.

Cameron, Iain. The Protective Principle of International Criminal Jurisdiction. London: Ashgate, 1994.

Chilcote, Ronald H. Theories of Comparative Politics: The Search for a Paradigm Reconsidered. Boulder: Westview Press, 1994.

Coquillette, Daniel R., ed. Law in Colonial Massachusetts, 1630-1800: A Conference held 6 and 7 November 1981 by the Colonial Society of Massachusetts. Boston: Colonial Society of Massachusetts, 1984.

Coulton, George Gordon. Inquisition and Liberty. Boston: Beacon Press, 1959.

Curtis, Michael, ed. Introduction to Comparative Government. 3rd ed. New York: HarperCollins College Publishers, 1993.

Danziger, James N. Understanding The Political World: A Comparative Introduction to Political Science. 2nd ed. White Plains, NY: Longman, 1994.

David, Rene, and Brierley, John E.C. Major Legal Systems in the World Today. London: Stevens & Sons, 1985.

Del Carmen, Rolando V. Criminal Procedure: Law and Practice. 2nd ed. Pacific Grove, CA: Brooks/Cole Publishing Company, 1987.

Dudley, William, ed. The Creation of the Constitution: Opposing Viewpoints. American History Series. San Diego, CA: Greenhaven Press, 1995.

Dunham, Roger G., and Alpert, Geoffrey P. Critical Issues in Policing: Contemporary Readings. Prospect Heights, IL: Waveland Press, Inc., 1989.

Dunn, John. The Political Thought of John Locke: An Historical Account of The Argument of The "Two Treatises of Government". Cambridge: Cambridge University Press, 1969.

Editors of Encyclopaedia Britannica. Law In America: How and Why It Works. New York: Bantam Books, 1979.

Elton, Geoffrey R. Star Chamber Stories. London: Methuen & Co. Ltd., 1983.

Epstein, Lee, and Walker, Thomas G. Constitutional Law for a Changing America: Rights, Liberties, and Justice. Washington, DC: CQ Press Division of Congressional Quarterly Inc., 1992.

Finch, Henry, Sir. A Summary of the Common Law of England. London: 1654; Wingate, Edmund. The Body of the Common Law of England. London: 1655; Phillipps, William. The Principles of Law Reduced to Practice London: 1660; reprint ed. of 3 works, New York: Garland, 1979.

Gardner, Thomas J., and Anderson, Terry M. Criminal Evidence: Principles and Cases. 3rd ed. St. Paul, MN: West Publishing Company, 1995.

Goebel, Julius, and Naughton, T. Raymond. Law Enforcement in Colonial New York: A Study in Criminal Procedure (1664-1776).Montclair, NJ: Patterson Smith, 1970.

Gray, Jeffrey. The Psychology of Fear and Stress. New York: McGraw-Hill Book Co., 1971.

Hagan, Frank E. Research Methods in Criminal Justice and Criminology. 2nd ed. New York: Macmillan Publishing Company, 1989.

Hale, Matthew, Sir. The History of the Common Law of England. Introduction by Charles M. Gray, ed. Chicago: University of Chicago Press, 1971.

Hall, Calvin S., and Lindzey, Gardner. Theories of Personality. 3rd ed. New York: John Wiley & Sons, 1978.

Hauss, Charles. Comparative Politics: Domestic Responses to Global Challenges. St. Paul, MN: West Publishing Company, 1994.

Hartog, Hendrik, ed. Law in the American Revolution and the Revolution in the Law: A Collection of Review Essays on American Legal History, New York University School of Law Series in Legal History, no. 3. New York: New York University Press, 1981.

Hawles, Sir J. Justices and Juries in Colonial America: Two Accounts, 1680-1722. American Law: The Formative Years Series. New York: Arno Press, 1972.

Heath, James. Torture and English Law: An Administrative and Legal History from the Plantagenets to the Stuarts. Contributions in Legal Studies, No. 18. Westport, CT: Greenwood Press, 1982.

Hoffer, Peter Charles. Law and People in Colonial America. Baltimore: John Hopkins University Press, 1992.

Howland, Arthur C., ed. Translations and Reprints From the Original Sources of European History. Philadelphia, PA: The Department of History of the University of Pennsylvania, 1898. Vol. 4: Ordeals, Compurgation, Excommunication and Interdict.

Hroch, Miroslav, and Skybova, Anna. Ecclesia Militans: The Inquisition. Translated by Janet Fraser. Dorset Press, 1990.

Huntington, Samuel P. Political Order in Changing Societies. New Haven and London: Yale University Press, 1968.

Kamisar, Yale et al. Basic Criminal Procedure. St. Paul, MN.: West Publishing Co., 1994.

Kamisar, Yale; LaFave, Wayne R.; and Israel, Jerold H. Modern Criminal Procedure: Cases, Comments and Questions. 7th ed. St. Paul, MN: West Publishing Co., 1990.

Klein, Irving J. Constitutional Law for Criminal Justice Professionals. Vol. 2, 2nd ed. Miami, FL: Coral Gables Publishing Co., 1986.

_____. 1989 Supplement to Constitutional Law for Criminal Justice Professionals. 2nd ed., Miami, FL: Coral Gables Publishing Co., 1989.

_____. 1990 Supplement to Constitutional Law for Criminal Justice Professionals. 2nd ed., Miami, FL: Coral Gables Publishing Co., 1990.

Klotter, John C., and Kanovitz, Jacqueline R. Constitutional Law. 6th ed. Justice Administration Legal Series. Cincinnati, OH: Anderson Publishing Co., 1991.

Kocourek, Albert, and Wigmore, John H., comps. Evolution of Law: Select Readings on the Origin and Development of Legal Institutions. Boston: Little, Brown, and Company, 1915. Vol. II: Primitive and Ancient Legal Institutions.

Langbein, John H. Torture and the Law of Proof: Europe and England in the Ancien Regime. Chicago: The University of Chicago Press, 1977.

Lea, Henry Charles. Torture. Philadelphia: University of Pennsylvania Press, Inc., 1973.

Lilburn, John. Londons Liberty: In Chains Discovered. London: By the author, Tower of London, 1646.

Lobban, Michael. The Common Law and English Jurisprudence, 1760-1850. Oxford, England: Clarendon Press, 1991.

Locke, John. An Essay Concerning Human Understanding. 2 vols. 17th ed. London: For John Beecroft, No. 23, Pater-noster-Row, 1775.

Locke, John. Two Treatises of Government. Edited by Peter Laslett. Cambridge: Cambridge University Press, 1988.

Lykken, David Thorson. A Tremor in the Blood: Uses and Abuses of the Lie Detector. New York: McGraw-Hill, 1981.

Mace, George. Locke, Hobbes, and the Federalist Papers: An Essay on the Genesis of the American Political Heritage. Carbondale and Edwardsville: Southern Illinois University Press, 1979.

Macridis, Roy C., and Burg, Steven L. Introduction to Comparative Politics: Regimes and Change. 2nd ed. New York: HarperCollins Publishers Inc., 1991.

Madison, James; Hamilton, Alexander; and Jay, John. The Federalist: A Collection of Essays, Written in Favour of the New Constitution, as Agreed Upon by the Federal Convention, September 17, 1787. New York: J. and A. McLean, 1788; reprint ed., The Federalist Papers. Introduction by Isaac Kramnick. New York: Penguin Books, 1987.

Mahler, Gregory S. Comparative Politics: An Institutional and Cross-National Approach. Englewood Cliffs, NJ: Prentice-Hall, Inc., 1995.

Mason, Alpheus Thomas; Beaney, William M.; and Stephenson, Donald Grier, Jr. American Constitutional Law: Introductory Essays and Selected Cases. 7th ed. Englewood Cliffs, NJ: Prentice-Hall, Inc., 1983.

Maxwell, W. Harold, and Brown C.R. comps. A Complete List of British and Colonial Law Reports and Legal Periodicals: Arranged in Alphabetical and in Chronological Order with Bibliographical Notes: With a Check List of Canadian Statutes. 3rd ed. Toronto, Ont.: Carswell Co., 1937.

Meltzer, Milton. The Bill of Rights: How We Got It and What It Means. New York: Thomas Crowell, 1990.

Mendelson, Wallace. The American Constitution and Civil Liberties. Homewood, IL: The Dorsey Press, 1981.

Nass, Gilbert D.; Libby, Roger W.; and Fisher, Mary Pat. Sexual Choices: An Introduction to Human Sexuality. Monterey, CA: Wadsworth Health Sciences Division of Wadsworth, Inc., 1981.

O'Brien, David M. Constitutional Law and Politics. Vol. 1: Struggles for Power and Governmental Accountability. 2nd ed. New York: W.W. Norton & Company, 1995.

_____. Storm Center: The Supreme Court in American Politics. 2nd ed. New York: W.W. Norton & Company, 1990.

Parry, L.A. The History of Torture in England. Patterson Smith Series in Criminology, Law Enforcement, and Social Problems, No. 180. London: Sampson Low. Marston & Co., Ltd., 1934; reprint ed., Montclair, NJ: Patterson Smith Publishing Corporation, 1975.

Patterson, Thomas E. We the People: A Concise Introduction to American Politics. New York: McGraw-Hill, Inc., 1995.

Peltason, J.W. Corwin & Peltason's Understanding the Constitution. 11th ed. New York: Holt, Rinehart and Winston, Inc., 1988.

Pennypacker, Samuel Whitaker. Pennsylvania Colonial Cases: The Administration of Law in Pennsylvania prior to A.D. 1700 as shown in the Cases Decided and in the Court Proceedings. Philadelphia: R. Welsh, 1892.

Peters, Edward. Torture. New Perspectives on the Past Series. Oxford: Basil Blackwell Ltd., 1985; reprint ed., New York: Basil Blackwell Inc., 1986.

Plucknett, Theodore F.T. A Concise History of the Common Law 5th ed. Boston: Little, Brown and Company, 1956.

Reid, John E., and Inbau, Fred E. Truth and Deception: The Polygraph Technique 2nd ed. Baltimore: The Williams & Wilkins Company, 1977.

Rhyne, Charles S. Law and Judicial Systems of Nations. 3rd ed. Washington, DC: The World Peace Through Law Center, 1978.

Riechel, Philip L. Comparative Criminal Justice Systems: A Topical Approach. Englewood Cliffs, NJ: Prentice Hall Career & Technology, 1994.

Rose, Richard. Politics in England: Change and Persistence 5th ed. Little, Brown Series in Political Science. Glenview, IL: Scott, Foresman and Company, 1989.

Royal, Robert F., and Schutt, Steven R. The Gentle Art of Interviewing and Interrogation: A Professional Manual and Guide. Englewood Cliffs, NJ: Prentice-Hall, Inc., 1976.

Russell, Elmer Beecher. The Review of American Colonial Legislation by the King in Council. Historial Writings in Law and Jurisprudence Series. New York: Columbia University, 1915; reprint ed., Buffalo: W.S. Hein, 1981.

Ruthven, Malise. Torture: The Grand Conspiracy. London: Weidenfeld and Nicolson 1978.

Rutland, Robert Allen. The Birth of the Bill of Rights 1776-1791. Boston: Northeastern University Press, 1983.

Samaha, Joel. Criminal Procedure. 2nd ed. St. Paul, MN: West Publishing Company, 1993.

Scheb, John M., and Scheb, John M. II. Criminal Law and Procedure. 2nd ed. St. Paul, MN: West Publishing Company, 1993.

Scott, Arthur Pearson. Criminal Law in Colonial Virginia. Chicago, IL: The University of Chicago Press, 1930.

Scott, George Ryley. The History of Torture Throughout the Ages. London: T. Werner Laurie Ltd, 1940; reprint ed., Gateshead on Tyne: Northumberland Press Limited, 1941.

Selden Society. Select Cases Before the King's Council in The Star Chamber commonly called The Court of Star Chamber A.D. 1477-1509. London: Bernard Quaritch, 1903.

Seliger, M. The Liberal Politics of John Locke.. New York, NY: Frederick A. Praeger, Inc., 1969.

Selye, Hans. The Stress of Life. rev. ed. New York: McGraw-Hill Book Co., 1978.

Shively, W. Phillips. Power and Choice: An Introduction to Political Science. 4th ed. New York: McGraw-Hill Book Co., 1995.

Smith, P.F., and Bailey, S.H. The Modern English Legal System. London: Sweet & Maxwell, 1984.

Suedfeld, Peter, ed. Psychology and Torture. New York: Hemisphere Publishing Corp., 1990.

Taylor, Ralph B. Research Methods in Criminal Justice. New York: McGraw-Hill, Inc., 1994.

Terrill, Richard J. World Criminal Justice Systems: A Survey. 2nd ed. Cincinnati, OH: Anderson Publishing Co., 1992.

Ulmer, S. Sidney. Supreme Court Policymaking and Constitutional Law. New York: McGraw-Hill Book Company, 1986.

164

von Mehren, Arthur Taylor, and Gordley, James Russell. The Civil Law System. 2nd ed. Boston: Little, Brown and Company, 1977.

Waltz, Jon R. Introduction to Criminal Evidence. 3rd ed. Chicago: Nelson-Hall Publishers, 1991; reprint ed., 1992.

Weston, Paul B.; Wells, Kenneth M.; and Hertoghe, Marlene E. Criminal Evidence for Police. 4th ed. Englewood Cliffs, NJ: Prentice-Hall, Inc., 1995.

Wasby, Stephen L. The Supreme Court in the Federal Judicial System. 3rd ed. Chicago: Nelson-Hall Publishers, 1988; reprint ed., 1989.

Wigmore, John Henry. Evidence in Trials at Common Law vol. 3. Revised by James H. Chadbourne. Boston: Little, Brown and Company, 1970.

_____. A Kaleidoscope of Justice Containing Authentic Accounts of Trial Scenes from all Times and Climes. Washington, DC: Washington Law Book Co., 1941.

_____. A Pocket Code of the Rules of Evidence in Trials at Law. Massachusetts Edition by Charles N. Harris. Boston: Little, Brown and Company, 1915.

_____. The Principles of Judicial Proof as Given by Logic, Psychology, and General Experience. Boston: Little, Brown and Company, 1913.

_____. The Principles of Judicial Proof or The Process of Proof as given by Logic, Psychology, and General Experience and illustrated in Judicial Trials. 2nd ed. Boston: Little, Brown, and Company, 1931.

REPORTS - PUBLISHED

Amnesty International. Report on Torture. New York: Farrar, Straus and Giroux, 1974.

Gardner, J.P. Aspects of Incorporation of the European Convention of Human Rights into Domestic Law London: British Institute of International and Comparative Law, (1993).

ARTICLES IN JOURNALS OR MAGAZINES

Journal of Politics, Vol. 18 (1956): Almond, Gabriel, *'Comparative Political Systems.'*

Michigan Law Review, Vol. 93, No. 5 (March 1995): Amar, Akhil Reed, and Lettow, Renee B., *'Fifth Amendment First Principles: The Self-Incrimination Clause.'*

University of Michigan Journal of Law Reform Vol. 24, Issue 1 (Fall 1990): Berger, Mark, *'Legislating Confession Law in Great Britain: A Statutory Approach to Police Interrogations.'*

Harvard Law Review (106)1236 (March 1993): Bodenhamer, David J., *'Fair Trial: Rights of the Accused in American History.'*

American Journal of Comparative Law 41 (Spring 1993): Brzezinski, Mark F., *'The Emergence of Judicial Review in Eastern Europe: The Case of Poland.'*

Northwestern University Law Review Vol. 90, No. 2 (1996).Cassell, Paul G., *'Miranda's Social Cost: An Empirical Reassessment.'*

UCLA Law Review (43)001 (1996): Cassell, Paul G., and Hayman, Bret S., *'Police Interrogation in the 1990s: An Empirical Study of the Effects of Miranda.'*

Cornell Law Review 63 (1977): Craver, Charles B., *'The Inquisitorial Process in Private Employment.'*

Contemporary Crises Vol. 8, No. 3 (1984): DiChiara, Albert, and Galliher, John F., *'Thirty Years of Deterrence Research: Characteristics, Causes, and Consequences.'*

Anglo-American Law Review 20(1) (1991): Feldman, David; Jackson, Gordon; Dixon, David; and others. *'Criminal Investigation - Reform and Control.'*

Criminal Law Review (March 1993): Fenwick, H., *'Confessions, Recording Rules and Miscarriages of Justice: A Mistaken Emphasis?'*

The Catholic University Law Review (36)611 (Spring 1987).Geyh, Charles Gardner, *'The Testimonial Component of the Right against Self-Incrimination.'*

Michigan Law Review (92)1047 (1994): Langbein, John H., *'The Historical Origins of the Privilege Against Self-Incrimination at Common Law.'*

University of Cincinnati Law Review 53(1) (1984): LeFrancois, A.G., *'On Exorcising the Exclusionary Demons - An Essay on Rhetoric, Principle, and the Exclusionary Rule.'*

Georgia Journal of International and Comparative Law 23 (Summer 1993): Ludwikowski, Rett R., *'Constitution Making in the Countries of Former Soviet Dominance: Current Development.'*

Law and Order (January 1982): McKinnon, Murlene E,. *'A Guide to Nonverbal Deception Indicators.'*

'Journal of Crime and Justice Vol. 13, No. 1 (1990): Maguire, Brendan, *'The Police in the 1800s: A Three City Analysis.'*

American Scholar 55 (Summer 1986): Malone, Patrick A., *'"You have the Right to Remain Silent": Miranda after Twenty Years.'*

American Journal of Comparative Law 40 (Winter 1992): Manfredi, Christopher P., *'The Canadian Supreme Court and American Judicial Review: United States Constitutional Jurisprudence and the Canadian Charter of Rights and Freedoms.'*

Michigan Law Review (92)1086. Moglen, Eben, '*Taking the Fifth: Reconsidering the Origins of the Constitutional Privilege against Self-Incrimination.*'

Criminal Behaviour and Mental Health 3/1 (1993): Moston, S.; Stephenson, G.M.; and Williamson, T.M., '*The Incidence, Antecedents and Consequences of The Use of The Right to Silence During Police Questioning.*'

American Journal of Comparative Law 41 (Fall 1993): Sage, Yves-Louis, '*The 1990 French Laws on the Legal Profession.*'

Criminal Law Bulletin Vol. 15, No. 1 (Jan/Feb. 1979): Sherman, Lawrence W., '*Enforcement Workshop: The Boundaries of Interrogation.*'

National Law Journal (7 August 1989): Strasser, Fred, '*Perceptions and Reality; Crime in America.*'

Crimecare Journal Vol. 4, No. 2 (1988): Talbot, C.K., '*Towards a Criminology of Literature.*'

Judicature 77 (March/April 1994): Utter, Robert F., '*Comparative Aspects of Judicial Review: Issues facing the New European States.*'

Ohio State Law Journal 54, No. 3 (1993): _____. '*Judicial Review in the New Nations of Central and Eastern Europe: Some Thoughts from a Comparative Perspective.*'

The Hastings Law Journal Vol. 38:1 (Nov. 1986).Van Kessel, Gordon, '*The Suspect as a Source of Testimonial Evidence: A Comparison of the English and American Approaches.*'

The Police Chief (October 1979): Wicklander, Douglas E., '*Behavioral Interviews to a Confession.*'

Cornell International Law Journal 24 (Spring 1991): Young, Marianne Wilder, '*The Need for Legal Aid Reform: A Comparison of English and American Legal Aid.*'

Journal of Criminal Justice Education Vol. 1, No. 1 (1990): Young, Thomas J., '*Native American Crime and Criminal Justice Require Criminologists' Attention.*'

ARTICLES IN ENCYLOPEDIAS

Encyclopedia Americana - International Edition, '*Ordeal*' 1992.

Encyclopedia Americana - International Edition, "*Torture*' by Leonard D. Savitz.1992.

Encyclopaedia Britannica, Vol. 16. 14th ed. "*Ordeal.*'

Encyclopaedia of Religion, Vol. II. '*Ordeal*' by Dario Sabbatucci.

Encyclopaedia of Religion and Ethics, Vol. IX. *'Ordeal'* by A.E. Crawley; Th. W. Juynboll; S. Langdon; J.A. MacCulloch; R.F. Johnston; P. Vinogradoff; J.A. Selbie; A.B. Keith; E. Edwards; G. Grandidier; A.C. Pearson; and M.E. Seaton.

Encyclopedic Dictionary of Religion, *'Torture'* 1979.

NEWSPAPERS

Independent, 9.11.94.*'A Modern Enactment of the Star Chamber.*

Daily Telegraph, 8.20.94.*'A Few Words of Caution - The Right to Silence.'*

Independent, 8.20.94. Bennetto, Jason, *'New Police Caution Alarms Legal Experts.'*

Independent, 11.14.94.Brace, Matthew, *'Life with the Criminal Justice Act.'*

Reuter News Service -UK, 10.19.94. *'British Lawyers Criticise New Police Caution.'*

Hermes-UK Government Press Release, 11.18.94. *'Criminal Justice (Scotland) Bill Published.'*

Reuter New Service - UK, 5.17.94. *'Curbing Right to silence a Failure.'*

Daily Telegraph, 5.24.94. de Lisle, Charles, *'Right to Silence' Rebels Defeated.'*

The Age (Melbourne), 11.5.94. Ellingsen, Peter, *'Britain's New Law and Disorder.'*

The Times, 5.17.94. Ferguson, Richard, *'More of the Innocent will be at Risk - Right to Silence.'*

Independent, 11.29.94. *'In Judgment on the Government.'*

International Criminal Police Review, March 1978.

International Criminal Police Review, August/September 1978.

Sunday Times, 10.16.94. Kane, Frank, *'DTI Discredited - Business Focus.'*

South China Morning Post, 9.22.94. Kohli, Sheel, *'London Calling.'*

Independent, 1.14.94. *'Life with the Criminal Justice Act.'*

Daily Telegraph, 7.8.94. Looch, Anthony, *'Suspects to be Cautioned on Silence.'*

Glasgow Herald, 11.30.94. McGregor, Stephen, *'Clash Over Right to Silence for Accused.'*

Glasgow Herald, 10.28.94. McKain, Bruce, *'Scots Law Experts Question Need for Silence Rule Change.'*

Independent, 11.4.94. Mills, Heather, and Penman, Danny, *'Bill Ends its Stormy Passage into Law.'*

Independent, 11.17.94. *'The Queen's Speech - Scotland.'*

Economist, *'The Right to Silence - Criminal Justice Bill.'*

Daily Telegraph, 5.17.94. Shaw, Terence, *'Convictions Drop with the Removal of Right to Silence.'*

Guardian, 10.20.94. Travis, Alan, *'Howard Patches Battered Bill.'*

Independent, 5.20.94. Wynn-Davies, Patricia, *'Peers May Force Change on RIght to Silence.'*

THESES AND OTHER PAPERS

Kibitlewski, Joseph L. *'The Use of Psychology in Interrogation.'* Paper presented at the 55th annual meeting of the Mississippi Academy of Sciences, Jackson, MS., 22 February 1991.

Reinsch, Paul Samuel. *'English Common Law in the Early American Colonies.'* Thesis, Wisconsin University, 1899.

UNITED STATES GOVERNMENT DOCUMENTS

U.S. Army Land Warfare Laboratory. *'Final Report on Detection of Emotional Stress by Voice Analysis.'* Report No. LWL-CR-03B70. Aberdeen Proving Ground, Maryland. September 1972.

UNITED STATES LEGAL CITATIONS

Adamson v. California, 332 U.S. 46, 67 S. Ct. 1962, 91 L. Ed. 1093 (1947).

Alston v. United States, 383 A. 2d 307 (D.C. 1978).

Apodaca v. Oregon, 406 U.S. 404, 92 S. Ct. 1628, 32 L. Ed. 2d 184 (1972).

Argersinger v. Hamlin, 407 U.S. 25, 92 S. Ct. 2006, 32 L. Ed. 2d 530 (1972).

Ashcraft v. Tennessee, 322 U.S. 143, 64 Sup. Ct. 921, 88 L. Ed. 1192 (1944).

Baltimore City Department of Social Services v. Bouknight, 46 CRL 2096 (1990).

Bartkus v. Illinois, 359 U.S. 121, 79 S. Ct. 676, 2 L. Ed. 2d 684 (1959).

Beckwith v. United States, 425 U.S. 341, 96 S. Ct. 1612 (1976).

Betts v. Brady, 316 U.S. 455, 465, 62 S. Ct. 1252, 86 L. Ed. 1595 (1942).

Blair v. United States, 250 U.S. 273 (1919).

Breed v. Jones, 421 U.S. 519, 95 S. Ct. 1779, 44 L. Ed. 2d 346 (1975).

Brown v. Illinois, 422 U.S. 590, 95 S. Ct. 2254, 45 L. Ed. 2d 416 (1975).

Brown v. Mississippi, 297 U.S. 278, 56 Sup. Ct. 461, 80 L. Ed. 682 (1936).

Brown v. State, 576 S.W. 2d 36 (Tex. Crim. App. 1979).

Brown v. Walker, 161 U.S. 591 (1896).

Burch v. Louisiana, 441 U.S. 130, 99 S. Ct. 1623, 60 L. Ed. 2d 96 (1979).

California v. Beheler, 463 U.S. 1121, 103 S. Ct. 3517, L. Ed. 2d 1275 (1983).

California v. Byers, 402 U.S. 424, 464-65, 473-74 (1971).

Cardarell v. United States, 375 F. 2d 222 (8th Cir. 1967).

Chambers v. Florida, 309 U.S. 227, 60 S. Ct. 472, 84 L. Ed. 716 (1940).

Coleman v. Alabama, 399 U.S. 1 (1970).

Colorado v. Spring, 479 U.S. 564, 107 S. Ct. 851 (1987).

Counselman v. Hitchcock, 142 U.S. 547 (1892).

Daly v. Superior Court, 19 Cal. 3d 132, 137 Cal. Rptr. 14 (1975).

Daubert v. Merrel Dow Pharmaceuticals, 113 S. Ct. 2786. (1993).

Davis v. State, 501 S.W. 2d 629 (Tex. Crim. App. 1973).

Douglas v. California, 372 U.S. 353, 83 S. Ct. 814, 9 L. Ed. 2d 811 (1963).

Douglas v. Petrol Stops Northwest, 441 U.S. 221 (1979).

Elkins v. United States, 364 U.S. 206, 80 S. Ct. 1437, 4 L. Ed. 2d 1669 (1960).

Ellis v. United States, 416 F. 2d 801 (1969).

Escobedo v. Illinois, 378 U.S. 478, 488-491 (1964).

Estelle v. Williams, 425 U.S. 96 S. Ct. 1691, 48 L. Ed. 2d 126 (1976).

Faretta v. California, 422 U.S. 806, 95 S. Ct. 2525, 45 L. Ed. 2d 562 (1975).

Ferguson v. Georgia, 365 U.S. 570, 81 S. Ct. 756, 5 L. Ed. 2d 793 (1961).

Fitzpatrick v. United States, 178 U.S. 304 (1900).

Fong Foo v. United States, 369 U.S. 141, 82 S. Ct. 671, 7 L. Ed. 2d 629 (1962).

Frye v. United States, 293 Fed. 1013 (App. D.C. 1923).

Fuller v. Oregon, 417 U.S. 40 (1974).

Gallegos v. Colorado, 370 U.S. 49, 82 S. Ct. 1209 (1962).

Garner v. United States, 424 U.S. 648, 96 S. Ct. 1178 (1976).

Gideon v. Wainwright, 372, U.S. 335, 83 S. Ct. 792, 9 L. Ed. 2d 799 (1963).

Gilbert v. California, 388 U.S. 263 (1967).

Graves v. United States, 472 A. 2d 395 (D.C. 1984).

Green v. United States, 355 U.S. 184, 78 S. Ct. 221, 2 L. Ed. 2d 199 (1957).

Griffin v. California, 380 U.S. 609 (1965).

Grosso v. United States, 390 U.S. 62, 88 S. Ct. 709, 19 L. Ed. 2d 906 (1968).

Hamilton v. Alabama, 368 U.S. 52, 82 S. Ct. 157, 7 L. Ed. 2d 114 (1961).

Haynes v. Washington, 373 U.S. 503, 83 S. Ct. 1336, 10 L. Ed. 2d 513 (1963).

Hill v. State, 366 So. 2d 318 (Ala. 1979).

Hoffman v. United States, 341 U.S. 479 (1951).

Holt v. United States, 218 U.S. 245 (1910).

Hughes v. Mathews, 576 F. 2d 1250 (7th Cir. 1978).

Huntingdon v. Crowley, 414 P. 2d 382 (Cal. 1966).

In Re Gault, 387 U.S.L. 87 S. Ct. 1428, 18 L. Ed. 2d 527 (1967).

Johnson v. Zerbst, 304 U.S. 458, 58 S. Ct. 1019, 82 L. Ed. 1461 (1938).

Kastigar v. United States, 406 U.S. 441 (1972).

Kepner v. United States, 195 U.S. 100, 24 S. Ct. 797, 49 L. Ed. 114 (1904).

Kirby v. Illinois, 406 U.S. 682, 92 S. Ct. 1877, 32 L. Ed. 2d 411 (1972).

Lakeside v. Oregon, 435 U.S. 333, 55 L. Ed. 2d 319, 98 S. Ct. 1091 (1978).

Letsinger v. United States, 402 A 2d 411 (1979).

Mackey v. United States, 401 U.S. 667, 91 S. Ct. 1160, 28 L. Ed. 2d 404 (1971).

McNabb v. United States, 318 U.S. 332, 63 Sup. Ct. 608, 87 L. Ed. 819 (1943).

Maine v. Moulton, 54 L.W. 4039 (1985).

Mallory v. Hogan, 378 U.S. 1, 84 S. Ct. 1489, 12 L. Ed. 2d. 653 (1964).

Mallory v. United States, 354 U.S. 449, 77 Sup. Ct. 1356, 1 L. Ed. 2d. 1479 (1957).

Mapp v. Ohio, 367 U.S. 643, 655 (1961).

Marbury v. Madison, 5 U.S. 368, 2 L. Ed. 60 (1803).

Marchetti v. United States, 390 U.S. 39, 88 S. Ct. 697, 19 L. Ed. 2d 889 (1968).

Mempa v. Rhay, 389 U.S. 128, 88 S. Ct. 254, 19 L. Ed. 2d 336 (1967).

Michigan v. Mosely, 423 U.S. 96, 96 S. Ct. 321, 46 L. Ed. 2d 313 (1975).

Michigan v. Tucker, 417 U.S. 433, 94 S. Ct. 2357, 41 L. Ed. 2d 182 (1974).

Minnesota v. Murphy, 465 U.S. 420, 104 S. Ct. 1136 (1984).

Miranda v. Arizona, 384 U.S. 436, 86 Sup. Ct. 1602, 16 L. Ed. 2nd 644 (1966).

Moran v. Burbine, 475 U.S. 412, 433 n. 4 (1986).

Murphy v. Waterfront Commisssion, 378 U.S. 52 (1964).

Mustafa v. United States Parole Comm'n, 479 U.S. 953 (1986).

New York v. Quarles, 467 U.S. 649, 104 S. Ct. 2626 81 L. Ed. 2d 550 (1984).

Norris v. Alabama, 295 U.S. 587 (1935).

O'Malley v. United States, 285 F. 2d 733, 734 (6th Cir. 1961).

One Lot Emerald Cut Stones and One Ring v. United States, 409 U.S. 232, 93 S. Ct. 489, 34 L. Ed. 2d 438 (1972).

Oregon v. Bradshaw, 459 U.S. 966, 103 S. Ct. 292, 74 L. Ed. 2d. 276, 51 L.W. 4940 (1983).

Oregon v. Elstad, 470 U.S. 298, 105 S. Ct. 1285, 84 L. Ed. 2d 222 (1985).

Orozco v. Texas, 394 U.S. 324, 89 S. Ct. 1095 (1969).

172

Pennsylvania v. Muñiz, 58 L.W. 4817 (1990).

People v. Cassidy, 213 N.Y. 388 (1915).

People v. Dorado, 398 P. 2d (Cal.) 381 U.S. 937 (1965).

People v. Gonzales, 120 Misc. 2d 62, 465 N.Y.S. 2d 471 (1983).

People v. Portelli, 15 N.Y. 2d 235, 204 N.E. 2d 857, N.Y. 2d 931 (1965).

People v. Sloane, 143 Cal Rptr. 61 (Ct. App. 2d Dist. 1978).

People v. Thompson, 193 Cal. Rptr. 782 (1983); 145 Cal. App. 3d 918 (1983).

People v. Watkins, 259 N.W. 2d 381 (Mich. Ct. App. 1977).

Philibosian v. Superior Court of the County of Los Angeles, 149 Cal. App. 3d 941, 197 Cal. Rptr. 208 (1984).

Pillsbury v. Conboy, 103 S. Ct. 608 (1983).

Powell v. Alabama, 287 U.S. 45, 53 S. Ct. 55, 77 L. Ed. 2d 158 (1932).

Presser v. Illinois, 116 U.S. 252, 6 S. Ct. 580, 29 L. Ed. 615 (1886).

Schmerber v. California, 384 U.S. 757, 86 S. Ct. 1826, 16 L. Ed. 2d 908 (1966).

Schneckloth v. Bustamonte, 412 U.S. 218, 93 S. Ct. 2041 (1973).

Shepard v. Baron, 194 U.S. 553 (1903).

Smith v. United States, 337 U.S. 137 (1949).

South Dakota v. Neville, 459 U.S. 553 (1983).

State v. Cory, 62 Wash. 2d 371, 382 P. 2d 1019 (1963).

State v. Halcomb, 3 NCA 169, (Neb. 1993).

State v. Smith, 362 N.E. 2d 1239 (Ohio Ct. App. 1976).

State Ex Rel. Tucker v. Davis, 9 Okla. Crim. 94, 130 P. 962 (1913).

Stultz v. State, 500 S.W. 2d 853 (Tex. 1973).

Taylor v. Alabama, 247 U.S. 687, 102 S. Ct. 2664, 73 L. Ed. 2d 314 (1982).

Tehan v. United States ex rel. Shott, 382 U.S. 406, 415 (1966).

Trop v. Dulles, 356 U.S. 86, 78 S. Ct. 590, 2 L. Ed. 2d 630 (1958).

Twining v. New Jersey, 211 U.S. 78, 29 S. Ct. 14, 53 L. Ed. 97 (1908).

United States v. Addison, 498 F. 2d 741 (D.C. Cir. 1974).

United States v. Anderson, 450 A. 2d 446 (D.C. 1982).

United States v. Bruno, 333 F. Supp. 570 (E.D. Pa. 1971).

United States v. Hasting, 461 U.S.499, 103 S. Ct. 1974, 76 L. Ed. 2d 96 (1983).

United States v. Henry, 447 U.S. 264, 100 S. Ct. 2183 (1980).

United States v. Kilgus, 571 F. 2nd 508 (9th Cir. 1978).

United States v. Kuehn, 562 F. 2d 426 (7th Cir. 1977).

United States v. Licavoli, 604 F. 2d 613 (9th Cir. 1974).

United States v. Miranti, 253 F. 2d 135 (2d Cir. 1958).

United States v. Muniz, 684 F. 2d 634 (9th Cir. 1982).

United States v. Oliver North, 910 F.2d 843 (D.C. Cir).

United States v. Prewitt, 553 F.2d 1082, 1985-96 (7th Cir. 1977).

United States v. Read, 658 F. 2d 1225 (7th Cir. 1981).

United States v. Robinson, 42 CRL 3063 (1988).

United States v. Wade, 388 U.S. 218 (1967).

United States v. Warren, 373 A. 2d 874 (D.C. 1977).

United States v. Washington, 431 U.S. 181, 97 S. Ct. 1814 (1977).

United States v. Williams, 456 F. 2d 217 (5th Cir. 1972).

Vaughn v. United States, 364 A. 2d 1187 (D.C. 1976).

Victoria v. State, 522 S.W. 2d 919 (Tex. Crim. App. 1975).

Wallace v. Jeffries, 472 U.S. 38, 105 S. Ct. 2749, 86 L. Ed. 2nd 29 (1985).

Weeks v. United States, 232 U.S. 383, 34 S. Ct. 341, 58 L. Ed. 652 (1914).

Weems v. United States, 217 U.S. 349, 377, 30 S. Ct. 544, 553, 54 L. Ed. 793, 802 (1910).

174

West Virginia State Board of Education v. Burnette 319 U.S. 624, 63 S. Ct. 1178, 87 L. Ed. 1628 (1943).

Wolf v. Colorado, 338 U.S. 25, 69 S. Ct. 1359, 93 L. Ed. 1782 (1949).

Wong Sun v. United States, 371 U.S. 471, 83 S. Ct. 407, 9 L. Ed. 2d 441 (1963).

ENGLISH LEGAL CITATIONS

A (A Minor) (Paternity: Refusal of Blood Test), In re [1994], 2 FLR 463.

B v. B and E [1969], 1 WLR 1800; [1969] 3 All E.R. 1106, CA.

Burbury v. Jackson [1917], 1 KB 16, DC.

CA and Turner v. Blunden [1986], Fam 120, DC.

Daly v. General Medical Council [1952], 2 All E.R. 666, [1952] WN 413.

Director of Public Prosecutions v. Gordon [1990], RTR 71, DC.

Director of Public Prosecutions v. Warren [1993], RTR 58, 65F, HL(E).

Director of Public Prosecutions v. Winstanley [1993], RTR 222, DC.

Edge v. Director of Public Prosecutions [1993], RTR 146, DC.

Fox v. Chief Constable of Gwent [1985], RTR 337, HL(E).

Guinness PLC v. Saunders and others [1988], Court of Appeal (Civil Division).

Hayes v. Director of Public Prosecutions [1994], RTR 163, DC.

JS (A Minor) (Declaration of Paternity), In re [1981], Fam 22, [1981] 2 FLR 146, [1980] 3 WLR 984, [1980] 1 All E.R. 1061.

JW v. K (Proof of Paternity) [1988], 1 FLR 86.

Johnson v. Chief Constable of Surrey [1992], Court of Appeal (Civil Division).

Johnstone and others v. United Norwest Co-operatives Ltd. [1994], Court of Appeal (Civil Division).

L (An Infant), In re [1968], P 119; [1967] 3 WLR 1149; [1967] 2 All E.R. 1110; [1968] P 119; [1967] 3 WLR 1645; [1968] 1 All E.R. 20, CA.

Lam Chi-Ming and others v. The Queen [1991], 2 AC 212, [1991] 3 All E.R. 172, [1991] 2 WLR 1082, 93 Cr App Rep 358.

McVeigh v. Beattie [1988], Fam 69, [1988] 2 All E.R. 500, [1988] 2 WLR 992, [1988] 2 FLR 67, [1988] Fam Law 290.

Mash v. Darley [1914], 3 KB 1226, CA.

Mead v. Director of Public Prosecutions [1993], RTR 151, DC.

Morris v. Beardmore [1980], RTR 321, HL(E).

Murray v. Director of Public Prosecutions [1993], RTR 209, DC.

Ogburn v. Director of Public Prosecutions [1994], 1 WLR 1107, [1994] RTR 241, 1 Cr App Rep 383.

Paterson v. Director of Public Prosecutions [1990], RTR 329, DC.

Pine v. Collacott [1985], RTR 282.

Police v. Rajandah Coomar Kristnamah [1993], Privy Council.

Rank Film Distributors, Ltd. and others v. Video Information Centre and others. Court of Appeal (Civil Division) [1982] AC 380, [1980] 2 All E.R. 273, [1980] 3 WLR 487, [1970] FSR 242.

Reffell v. Morton [1906], 70 JP 347, DC.

Reg v. Absolam [1989], 88 Cr App Rep 336.

Reg v. Brine [1992], Crim LR 122.

Reg v. Brody House of Lords [1982], AC 476, [1981] All E.R. 705, [1983] 3 WLR 103, 73 Cr App Rep 287, 145.

Reg v. Chief Metropolitan Stipendiary Magistrate, Ex parte Secretary of State for the Home Department [1988] 1 WLR 1204; [1989] 1 All E.R. 151, DC.

Reg v. Cooke, [1994], 1 Cr App Rep 318.

Reg v. Flavell [1884], 14 QBD 364.

Reg v. Greenwich London Borough Council, Ex parte Lovelace (No 2), [1992] QB 155, [1991] 3 WLR 1015, [1992] 1 All E.R 679 CA.

Reg v. Hamand [1985], 82 Cr App Rep 65, [1985] Crim LR 375.

Reg v. Kelt, (Criminal Division) [1994] 2 All E.R. 780, 99 Cr App Rep 372.

Reg v. King [1983], 1 All E.R. 929, [1983] 1 WLR 411.

Reg v. Robb [1991], 93 Cr App Rep 161.

Reg v. Sang [1979], 2 All E.R. 1222 at 1246, [1980] Ac 402 at 455 per Lord Scarman.

Reg v. Smith (Robert William) [1985], 81 Cr App Rep 286, CA.

Reg v. Stipendiary Magistrates Ex parte Director of the Serious Fraud Office, Queens Bench Division.

Reg v. Tottenham Justices Ex parte ML [1985], 82 Cr App Rep 277.

Reg v. W (A minor) Court of Appeal (Civil Division).

Reg v. Williams (Mark Alexander), Court of Appeal (Criminal Division) 156 JP 776.

Reg v. Wood [1994], Crim LR 222.

S v. S; W v. Official Solicitor [1972], AC 24, [1970] 3 WLR 366, [1970] 2 All E.R. 107, HL.

Senat v. Senat [1965], P 172; [1965] 2 WLR 981; [1965] 2 All E.R. 705.

Serio v. Serio [1983], 4 FLR 756.

Simpson v. Collinson [1964], 2 QB 80; [1964] 2 WLR 387; [1964] 1 All E.R. 262, CA.

Sociedade Nacional de Combustiveis de Angola UEE and others v. Lundquist and others. Court of Appeal (Civil Division) [1991] 2 QB 310, [1990] 3 All E.R. 283, [1991] 2 WLR 280.

Taylor and another v. Plymouth Argyle Football Co. Ltd. [1991], Court of Appeal (Civil Division).

Thomas v. Jones [1921], 1 KB 22, CA.

Turner v. Blunden [1986], Fam 120; [1986] 2 WLR 491; [1986] 2 All E.R. 75, DC.

W v. W (otherwise L) [1912], P 78.

Wong Kam-ming v. The Queen [1980], AC 247, [1979] 1 All E.R. 939, [1979] 2 WLR 81, 69 Cr App Rep 47.

Young v. Bristol Aeroplane Co. Ltd. [1944], KB 718, [1944] 1 all E.R. 293, CA.

INDEX

CRIMINOLOGY STUDIES